# ACCESSING
# ANCIENT
# PORTALS

# ACCESSING
# ANCIENT
# PORTALS

*Unlocking the Hebraic Foundations of Faith to*
## EXPERIENCE THE
## SUPERNATURAL!

## DR. SHARON R. NESBITT

DESTINY IMAGE® PUBLISHERS, INC.

PO Box 310, Shippensburg, PA 17257-0310

"Publishing cutting-edge prophetic resources to supernaturally empower the body of Christ"

This book and all other Destiny Image and Destiny Image Fiction books are available at Christian bookstores and distributors worldwide.

For more information on foreign distributors, call 717-532-3040.

Or reach us on the Internet: www.destinyimage.com

ISBN 13 TP: 978-0-7684-7751-1

ISBN 13EBook: 978-0-7684-7747-4

For Worldwide Distribution, Printed in the USA

1 2 3 4 5 6 / 26 25 24 23

*This book is dedicated to all those who have a passionate desire toward Abba Father, for you are the ones to whom He will give His hidden treasures.*

# CONTENTS

# ACCESSING ANCIENT PORTALS

Transcending dimensions is innate to the nature of a believer. As multi-dimensional beings, mankind has been empowered to serve as stewards over the Earth through his connection to heavenly realms. This is the supernatural link that provides the means by which amazing things can happen. Take miracles for instance, they happen because a connection exists between God and man. As I reflect on the many experiences I have had in life, I can see how drastically my level of understanding has shifted.

Growing up in a denominational church, we really didn't believe in healing according to the Word of God. We just believed that if it's the Lord's will, a person will be healed, if not, they would not. During the time of my mother's transition, we followed that mindset; "Lord if it be thy will, let my mom be healed." As it went, my mother, who was sick with cancer, did not survive. In response, it was said, "God chose to pick another rose from His garden." If we stop to think about it, a rose is a fragrant and beautiful thing. My mom was indeed very beautiful. Roses are associated with things that are delicate and desirable. At the time, it stood to reason that God would desire to take my mother home. When it comes to losing a loved one, we often think of heaven. What people sometimes forget is that we already dwell in heavenly places in Christ Jesus.

I'm astounded at how things can change from one generation to the next. I was 18 years old when my mother passed away. At the time, we didn't have the mind to look at things through the lens of the supernatural. After going from being reared in the church to serving 25 years in full-time ministry, I have discovered that there is a serious lack of understanding of the Kingdom of God, and its protocols and principles among believers. Years ago, we had the tradition of receiving the Word as it was given to us. We never challenged it. We did not take the initiative to investigate the context of what was being shared. If the leader said it, we just took what he or she said as absolute. Most of the time we didn't even bring our Bibles to church. Therefore, we were unable to follow along. We did have a Sunday School book, but we took what was written for face value. However, if we are going to be impactful for the Kingdom, we must encourage believers to study for themselves. Because pursuing greater revelations in Christ is the key to walking in higher dimensions.

Back then, I didn't have the understanding to know that miracles are the reality for those who choose to believe at a higher level, and I am also seeing the same today. One area where there has been a lack of under-standing is how to bring the Kingdom of God lifestyle into our daily lives.

So many people think that their way is the only way, but this is not the case. There is only one door, and that door is Jesus Christ, but there are many dimensions (levels of revelation) within Him. Isaiah 53 says, "by His stripes we are healed." He said He would put none of these diseases upon us. By His Word, we know that His healing is available to those who desire it.

One of the most profound healings that I can remember occurred as I was delivering a message at a church. A lady ran up to me and demanded that I heal her. She was suffering from a severe skin disease, the likes of which I had never seen before. Her face was disfigured with various lumps and bumps beyond my ability to describe them. I did not respond to her request immediately. I went on with the message, while thinking about what I should do. Again, the lady ran to the front; she grabbed the hem of my skirt demanding to be healed. At that moment, her act of faith opened a portal, and the healing Power of God became accessible. I accommodated her in accordance with the specifics of her request. She fell out under the power of the Spirit. When she got up, her skin was smooth. It had been totally regenerated by the healing power of God. When the people saw that she was healed, an explosion of excitement broke out. The people rejoiced greatly over the miracle they had witnessed. The portal stayed open and a five-week revival ensued. This is but one of hundreds of examples I could give of portals that have opened for miracles in our ministry. Let's be clear; this book is not about healing itself, but more about how accessing Ancient Portals can bring about the manifestation of God's power in our lives.

The spirits of religion and tradition has been working to block believers from deeper revelations in Christ. These spirits seek to ensure that people are devoid of understanding, thus relegating them to live a subpar existence. This is unacceptable. Not only are we called to experience the abundance that is in Christ, but we are also called to be "salt" and "light." We are called to demonstrate the Power of God through signs and wonders, that others may believe also.

The woman that received her healing demonstrates how a portal for healing opened by a single act of faith. But, did you know that the Father has given a prescribed system of continuous access to the heavenly dimension through Ancient Portals that are already open? Get excited because it's true, and by the time you finish this book, you will understand. The Ancient Portals that I am speaking of are hidden in the mysteries surrounding the Hebrew calendar, which encompasses The Sabbath and the Feasts of the Lord. I received a mandate to teach about it over 20 years ago. This book was birthed in response to that mandate and a two-hour intensive workshop titled "Accessing Ancient Portals: The Power of Faith, the Feasts, and First Fruits."

The response to the workshop was overwhelming. I was surprised to discover that many of the attendees had little or no understanding of what a portal is, how you can clearly find them all throughout scripture, and how they can be accessed biblically. There was also very little knowledge of God's calendar and system of giving that directly connects the believer with The Kingdom of God lifestyle. Therefore, the goals of this book include:

- providing a clear understanding of how God intends for His people to live by uncovering hidden portals in His Word;

- helping readers understand their Hebraic roots and how this applies to daily life;
- encouraging the Body of Christ to honor the appointed times as established in the scripture; and
- helping believers manifest the Kingdom economy using simple biblical principles.

Once understood and welcomed, these teachings will shift you from the stress, labor, and anxiety, that is often experienced in this world's system, and you will begin to move into new levels of peace, prosperity, and power!

# INTRODUCTION

I t's the epic challenge. A claustrophobic feeling. A glass ceiling that separates the richness of Heaven from an impoverished Earth. Really, it's not that dramatic, but it is real: the sense of ever searching for a way to actualize God's divine plan, in the fulfilling and abundant way that is so much a part of God's nature.

There is a way to unlock destiny, and it's not as hard as some might think. But first things first . . . For starters, we must come to terms with the primary dimensions of God. His existence encompasses the physical and spiritual. His vastness is incomprehensible. It's also a good idea for us to take note of God's personality. God is love, and He is preoccupied with the idea of unifying His creation with Himself by means of giving and receiving. For Him, this is an intimate exchange that results in multiplication. This is the revelation of the Kingdom in my own words. Christ taught His disciples to pray, "Our Father which art in heaven, hallowed be thy Name. Thy kingdom come, Thy will be done, in earth, as it is in heaven" (Matthew 6:9-10). In a few short words, let's just say that God desires to bring the spirit and the natural together for the upbuilding of His Kingdom. The day is soon to come when all of creation will say, "The kingdoms of this world have become the kingdoms of our Lord."

We are the vessels that He has entrusted to bring His grand vision to pass. Imagine that! Can you hear His voice? . . . (YOUR NAME) come up here, come up higher. I have mysteries and revelations for you. The time is short. Come fulfill my purposes. I have a plan, and that plan includes you. Did you hear that? Was it like thunder or was it a still small voice? However, He speaks to you, that's great. Just know that you are His secret weapon; you are the Trojan Horse! Yes, the Kingdom is now on Earth; it's hidden in the hearts of believers.

> **"And when he was demanded of the Pharisees, when the kingdom of God should come, he answered them and said, The kingdom of God cometh not with observation: Neither shall they say, Lo here! or, lo there! for, behold, the kingdom of God is within you."**
>
> LUKE 17:20B-21 KJV

Christ said that the Kingdom has already come. He was speaking of Himself. Today, Christ lives in those of us who believe in Him. Now that we know the Kingdom has come and that it is inside of us, we must come to a greater understanding of the Kingdom. This includes the innumerable technologies of the Kingdom. It is for this reason that God has led you to this book. He is going to illuminate your spirit with the understanding necessary to access Heaven by way of Ancient Portals for His divine purpose and Glory.

# Everything in Heaven and Earth is yours!

It is the Father's good pleasure to give you the kingdom according to Luke 12:32. The Kingdom is literally everything that God possesses in the natural and the spiritual. When I say He has given you everything, I mean everything, including everything that is in Heaven and everything that is in the Earth. This is the very first revelation that we must embrace as our reality in order to come into a fuller understanding of our inheritance as believers.

> (Christ) is the image of the invisible God, the firstborn of every creature: For by him were all things created, that are in heaven, and that are in earth, visible and invisible, whether they be thrones, or dominions, or principalities, or powers: all things were created by him, and for him: And he is before all things, and by him all things consist.
>
> COLOSSIANS 1:15-17

> For it pleased the Father that in Him (Christ) should all fullness dwell; And, having made peace through the blood of his cross, by him to reconcile all things unto himself; by him, I say, whether they be things in earth, or things in heaven.
>
> COLOSSIANS 1:19-20

These scriptures speak of a great mystery. It reveals that Christ is the embodiment of God, and that Christ is God. All fullness (everything in Heaven and Earth) is in Him. It shows us that God manifested Himself in bodily form for the purpose of reconciling everything back to Himself.

. . . in the dispensation of the fulness of times He might gather together in one all things in Christ, both which are in heaven, and which are on earth; even in Him: in whom also we have obtained an inheritance . . .

EPHESIANS 1:10-11A

It is important to note that scripture proves all things are in Christ, including our inheritance. Our inheritance became available to us when Christ shed his blood on the cross. It was then that the greatest portal of reconciliation was created in the history of man's existence, whereby we have been given all things.

This is the first takeaway we must grasp as we delve into the spiritual technologies of Ancient Portals.

## Understanding Ancient Portals

### Dimensions and Realms

Dimensions are planes of existence. Some planes have no boundaries; others are contained within the scope of time and space. A dimension is characterized by the reality that exists on that plane. For example, Heaven is the dimension of the spirit world. Therefore, it is characterized by the spiritual nature that dominates that dimension. Earth is the dimension of the natural world. Therefore, Earth is characterized by the natural nature that dominates that plane. Note, the terms "dimension," "plane," and "world" can be used interchangeably at times.

There are many realms within each dimension, and there are realms within realms. A realm is a territory that is controlled by the authority of a sovereign ruler such as a king. A realm is defined by the rules of the King.

Note, generally, the terms "kingdom" and "realm" are interchangeable.

## Portals

Portals are openings between Heaven and Earth, the spirit world and the natural world. They are access points called "doors" or "gates" that segue into spiritual and natural dimensions and realms.

## Doors and gates

A door is a movable barrier that allows ingress into or egress out of an enclosure. Doors speak to granting or denying one access to a person, an organization, an institution, a structure, a circumstance, or a level of enlightenment such as wisdom, knowledge or understanding. Doors often refer to entering or leaving enclosed spaces such as buildings or rooms. Jesus said,

> I am the door: by me if any man enter in, he shall be saved, and shall
> go in and out, and find pasture.
> JOHN 10:9

On the other hand, a gate opens or closes a road or pathway. Gates speak to direction, purpose, and destiny. Gates often refer to open spaces such as cities or pastures.

Both doors and gates speak of experiences such as life or death, success or failure, prosperity or lack, fulfillment or disappointment, progress or regression, reward or punishment, etc. The difference is that a door is a specific inflection point that leads to a specific reality, whereas a gate opens to a journey, in a sense, that culminates at a specific destination.

Enter ye in at the strait gate: for wide is the gate, and broad is the way, that leadeth to destruction, and many there be which go in thereat:

MATTHEW 7:13

# Accessing Ancient Portals

The subject of portals encompasses many things such as physically traveling in the spirit or natural, as well as gaining access to something that may be spiritual or natural without traveling to that place. Portals also relate to accessing things that may be tangible or intangible. The purpose of the revelations that are being revealed in this book is to help you receive all that is necessary for the fulfillment of your God-given purpose while living the abundant life that God has ordained. The following is an example of traveling through portals to access the blessings of God.

I have had a reoccurring vision during times of prayer in which I am taken up to another dimension where there are holding places full of blessings. In a particular vision, I saw replacement body parts. Some were labeled with names. Others had no names and were just spare parts that were there to be used by anyone who might need them. They could receive them by Faith. This dimension is not limited by space. Everything is brightly illuminated with a white light. As my eyes focused, things came into color. The array of colors were such that we have not experienced here on Earth. In this case, it is "prayer" that serves as the portal through which I was taken up to Heavenly places. Not all experiences happen like this. Out of body experiences, while in prayer, is but one example of the unlimited ways that God gives His people access to different realms and dimensions.

The Bible says that we live in a Kingdom. It says that the Kingdom is in us. The Bible also likens us to a city. Everything that a Kingdom or a city consists of exists in this place, which I believe is within you. This is the mystery of God in you and you in God. We have a natural connection to the spirit dimension, but because of Adam's fall, we are now required to access the dimensions and realms that are within God through portals. Jesus is the door to the Father. He is now the link between Earth and Heaven. As we boldly exercise our rights as Kingdom citizens, we must do so by faith in Jesus' name.

## Disclaimer

The Apostle Paul said, "For now we see through a glass, darkly; but then face to face: now I know in part; but then shall I know even as also I am known" (I Corinthians 13:12). The Kingdom of God is infinite, and it is ever increasing. Like Paul, I acknowledge the vast nature of the Kingdom. We know in part, and we prophesy in part. Never-the-less, we do know that it is given unto us to know the mysteries of the Kingdom. This book does not cover information pertaining to every portal that exists, as they are innumerable. Rather, it will provide valuable insights into the times and seasons of God and how they are designed to provide continuous access to the things of God.

Thank you for sharing in the revelation of Ancient Portals.

CHAPTER ONE

# KINGDOM CONCEPTS

*This book reveals how accessing Ancient Portals can heighten your passion and desire for God when your obedience comes from a place of love.*

The revelation of Ancient Portals began to unfold for me approximately 22 years ago from the time of the writing of this book. I was in prayer when God spoke to me about teaching His people regarding the Hebraic roots of our Faith.

**Def.: Hebraic**

adjective

1. of, relating to, or characteristic of the Hebrews or their language or culture.

Christian scholars believe that Hebrew was the original language of man.[1] Hebrew is also considered to be a living language[2] that possesses an innately supernatural and creative element. The Hebrew language is unique from any other language known to man. Each letter of the Hebrew alphabet is characterized by a symbol and a number, giving it a deeper meaning than other languages. In considering the implications surrounding the history of the Hebrew people and their language, we can make the connection between us as believers back to Abraham, Isaac, and Jacob, and possibly Adam and even the origins of the name of God.

Though there were so many deep and powerful revelations to excavate out of the Hebraic roots of our faith, I resisted God's call to teach on the topic. "Father," I contested, "The people will not receive what I have to say. They are in love with their festivals and their religious ways – they will only resist everything You want me to tell them." But, God insisted that I share this message, and I obeyed.

Sure enough, people did come against me for teaching about the Hebraic roots, but God insulated me. Even though we were going through the fire, we didn't feel the heat. We just kept on doing what God called us to do. As I continued to be obedient to God's mandate to teach His people, we prospered greatly. And, as Abba Father would have it, the very persons who persecuted us are now teaching their congregations some of the same things I was teaching back then.

My prayer is that we all realize that God has provided a way for His people to not only experience the sporadic opening of the heavens; He has also provided a system by which we can live in a continuous cycle of blessings. Jewish people understand the principles of adhering to God's system, and because of this, they are the most prosperous of any people on Earth.

Before we delve into the details of the revelation, there are some preliminary concepts necessary for us to understand.

# Concept 1

*To access the Kingdom, we must have a heart toward God.*

Have you ever heard the adage, "good intentions pave the way to hell?" I don't know if you've ever taken the time to think about what it means, so let me tell you a story that will demonstrate the point. This story is about a man who died and went to hell. When he arrived inside the gates of hell, the first thing he noticed was one particular imp. He was a gnarly looking thing with fangs and claws, hairy legs, dog ears and glowing eyes. Beside being the most utterly repulsive looking thing the man had ever seen, the imp had a very disturbing smirk on his face. It was like the expression of a trickster who had accomplished his ultimate deceit. The man was puzzled and horrified all at the same time. "My God!" the man cried as he collapsed onto his knees and dropped his head into his face. The imp leaped with glee, jumping all around this poor man's condemned soul as the man sobbed. The man looked up toward Heaven, and for the first time there was no heaven, only darkness, screams, and the putrid smell of sulfur. For this man, time was no more. There was only terror. Ten times, a hundred times, what seemed like a million times, the man cried out, "What have I done? Why am I here?" The more the man cried, the more the awful demon danced.

In a strange way, the man found the imp a bit comforting; it was as if he was someone he had known before. It was the incessant dancing that seemed so familiar. Eerily, the imp began to speak as he taunted the man. "My friend, my friend, my friend," he whispered in a hiss. It was then the man knew! That was the voice that the man had heard speaking through his many friends when he was alive, a time that felt light years away.

You see, the man's weakness was his desire to be accepted. He was the guy that everyone loved. He was the person who never met a stranger. Adored by all, the man made every appeasement to maintain his status among people. In his heart, he felt a longing to read his Bible; instead, he took on extra projects at work, requiring him to commit to longer hours. He promised himself he would read his Bible later. Later never came. Everyone loved him at his workplace; they could always count on him to get the job done, no matter what! For years his wife would beg, "Honey, let's take time for worship. Let's take time for the things of the Lord." He thought, "I wish she'd stop nagging me." He spent his weekends on the golf course with his friends. He attended countless meetings with his civic groups and clubs. During Christmas, Easter, Halloween, and other celebrations, he would go from gathering to gathering; this guy was truly the life of the party! He was most definitely the man about town. His life looked perfect, but secretly his family felt neglected, and so did God. Holy Spirit would visit him, speaking to him during quiet times, which were few and far between. He wouldn't listen. He was more interested in following the crowd. Truth be told, he was merely trying to compensate for the evil spirit of low self-esteem that had him bound. He was literally opening portals of death through his daily activities. Time went by and he never turned to God. Now, here he was, reduced to a heap of grief and regret. He'd become no more than an object of entertainment for the very demon who had tricked him into believing that his friends and acquaintances could make him feel better about himself. He'd taken the bait. Out of selfish motives, the man chose to believe that being seen as "the good guy" would, in reality, make him a good person. Sadly, he'd always had good intentions; but, it was his "good intentions" that landed him in hell.

Why did I tell you that story? The truth is that many people are so distracted by selfish desires that they never find the path to life eternal. They do things in the name of "faith" or trying to be "a good person" or even in the name of "Christianity" in an effort to do what they think is right outside of a sincere love for God. Like this man's "good intentions," their good deeds coupled with selfish motives only serve to open the gate that will ultimately lead them to hell. The Lord said, "Many will say to me in that day, Lord, Lord, have we not prophesied in thy name? and in thy name have cast out devils? and in thy name done many wonderful works? And then will I profess unto them, I never knew you: depart from me, ye that work iniquity" (Matthew 7:22-24).

As we explore Ancient Portals, we are exploring ways to reach Heaven, and ways to connect to the love of God! Before I start to share some of the mysteries of the Kingdom with you, I want you to look deep into your heart. Why are you reading this book? Why do you desire to understand the mysteries of the Kingdom? Of course, you desire to connect to the hidden riches that are in God. You desire to escape the curse and experience His blessings! But, know this,

## You will never enter into God's rest until you honestly desire to have intimacy with Him, which comes only through Jesus Christ.

The book of Genesis states that Adam "knew" his wife. God desires to know you, and He wants you to have that same desire for Him. When it says that Adam "knew" Eve his wife, it means that he had intimacy with her. Their relationship provides a clear picture of spiritual alignment with God! If you remember nothing else about this teaching on Ancient Portals,

## Remember that everything done in the Spirit of Love and obedience to God to open a portal between you and God is simply an act of alignment that creates the intimacy that God desires.

The man who went to hell was so busy trying to fulfill his desire for friendship with people that he got tricked into neglecting his friendship with God. Another thing that this book will teach you is that **there is no neutral place in the spirit**! Either you are aligning with the Kingdom of God or you're aligning with the kingdom of darkness. There is no middle ground.

The man in the story had good intentions. He was spending all his time trying to be the "good guy." In reality, his motives were impure. His desires were selfish and not toward God. He wanted to be important. He wanted to be seen of men, . . . and, to hell he went!

This is how the Pharisees were in the Bible. They did a lot of things to make themselves appear as "righteous" and "holy." There are 613 commandments in the Jewish tradition, and there is no way that anyone can keep them all. Yet, the Pharisees saw fit to flaunt their spirituality. "Look at me," they said in their hearts. "I'm righteous because I observe the weekly Sabbath, the monthly Sabbath, all the feasts. I give tithes and offerings, and I give to the poor. Look at me, I'm clean and you other people are nothing more than trifling wretches." This was their stinky attitude. The Bible says that they were as a dish, clean on the outside but filthy on the inside, full of dead men's bones. What that means is they condemned other people instead of helping them to know the unfailing love of God.

They understood the concept of alignment by way of keeping the sacred ordinances, but they didn't understand the love and passion that God has for us and the love and passion He desires from us. It was the very religious acts that they did, which alienated them from the God that they were pretending to serve. You must not allow these teachings to become legalistic.

This book will reveal to you how accessing Ancient Portals can actually heighten your passion and desire for God when your obedience comes from a place of love.

# Concept 2

*Pride mixed with revelation will bring destruction.*

The downfall of satan was pride. In line with this fact, let me interject this warning. There are so many who break through to a higher dimension of understanding. In doing so, they learn to traverse many realms. Some learn to tap into realms of healing, some realms of wealth, others realms of wisdom, and so on. By adding revelation to their gifts, they develop the ability to go in and out of realms at will by placing a demand on the Spirit of God through Faith. Still, in their humanity, many fall into temptation. Let's look at what the Apostle Paul had to say about this.

> "Know ye not that they which run in a race run all, but one re-ceiveth the prize? So run, that ye may obtain. And every man that striveth for the mastery is temperate in all things. Now they do it to obtain a corruptible crown; but we an incorruptible. I therefore so run, not as uncertainly; so fight I, not as one that beateth the air: But I keep under my body, and bring it into subjection: lest that by any means, when I have preached to others, I myself should be a castaway."
>
> I CORINTHIANS 9:24-27

In context, the Apostle Paul is speaking of the power and freedom that comes through the Gospel of Jesus Christ. He goes on to describe how he has willingly submitted to the call of preaching the Gospel in the spirit of humility. Next, he discusses the need for discipline to obtain His reward. The two points I would like to draw on are the need for submission and humility to avoid the pitfalls of temptation.

## Submission

Every believer has a calling on his or her life. Though there will be a price for us to pay, at some point, we must submit to the will of God. I submitted to His mandate to spread this message over two decades ago. At the risk of being ostracized, I chose the path of obedience. As the power of God's revelation is opened to us, we must know that it is ultimately for His glory and for our good.

## Humility

The Apostle Paul said that he humbled himself to do what was necessary to win as many souls as he could. He disciplined himself. There is a discipline of humility that is important to master so that we may stay grounded when the blessings of God begin to manifest in and through our lives.

I have resolved that I am nothing without God! I like the safety that comes with being in right standing with Him. I promised Him that if He would give me the grace to stay humble, I would allow Him to do the exalting. The power belongs to Him. The Glory is His; it does not belong to me. I so honor and love Him. Why? Because I do not desire just any reward; I desire His "great reward," which is my eternal reward that is in Him. Humility and the right focus are powerful technologies. When we put our focus on the things of the higher dimension, we will not succumb to the ills of the lower dimension.

When speaking of humility, honor for God goes along with that. The Spirit of the Fear of the Lord is honor. Honor is a place where we can dwell that opens portals into realms of promotion, advancement and increased favor, power, and dominion. When we walk in honor toward God, we will live in a more elevated place, according to His Word that says, *whatever a man sows, that shall he also reap.*

As you receive the revelation of how to access ancient portals, you will access realms of greater blessings. These blessings can cause a person to be prideful and even fall into sin if that person is not careful to stay focused on what He has called them to do. By submitting to His will, we will not fall into carnality. And, by walking in humility and honor toward God, we will continue to go from Glory to Glory in Him, not taking any credit for ourselves.

# Concept 3

*Understanding God's original intent helps provide insight.*

We're about to excavate some strategies, some portals, some realms, and some dimensions and open some ancient portals for the purpose of doing what God has called us to do in the Earth.

**Def.: portal**

noun

1. A doorway, entrance, or gate, especially one that is large and imposing.
2. An entrance or a means of entrance.
3  The portal vein.

Did you know that some of the basic tenets of our faith are actual portals into the spiritual dimension?   Such tenets include worship, altars, sacrifices, prayer, belief in Jesus Christ, the Blood of Jesus, faith, holiness, the Word of God, baptism, the infilling of the Holy Ghost, acts of righteousness, and alms.  The fall of man precipitated the need for portals.  Before Adam fell, man was in alignment with God, having full access to Him. Man was created to be a supernatural, multi-dimensional being who possessed the power to speak directly to God and to God's creation.  It was the sin of Adam that caused man to fall from the dimension where he had dominion with God. Portals, which are essentially systems and methods of alignment that act as doorways and gates to the things of God, were not a part of the original design. But, with the fall of man, portals (points of reconnection) became a necessity.  You will learn more in the chapters that follow.

As a sidebar, please note that as you are following along, you may be wondering what the significance of the word "Ancient" is.  When the word ancient is used, it is referencing the system of access to the supernatural dimension, which became a necessary technology after the fall of Adam thousands of years ago.

## God's original intent for man

To the point at hand, let us review God's original intent for man. The Bible says in Genesis that God created the *hashamayim*, which is the Hebrew term for the heavens and the Earth. These are two primary dimensions with which mankind is associated. In each of the two dimensions are levels or planes, which are also dimensions.  Within each dimension are many realms or kingdoms. An example is the animal kingdom, which is divided into sub-kingdoms called phylums and so on. Every kingdom must have a king or a sovereign ruler. Adam was the ruler of all kingdoms within the earthly dimension through God's delegated authority.

When contextualizing the book of Genesis, it can be surmised that originally God desired to have a family, superior representatives who would be a reflection of Himself in the Earth. Thus, He created man. He designed man to operate just like Him, to look and sound like him. Man was designed to operate in the attributes, the anointing, and the graces of who God is within the realms of the supernatural, which is our natural habitat, as man is a spirit. Man was designed to literally mirror God in the Earth dimension as well, as man is also a physical being. The first man and woman, Adam and Eve, fell from grace. When this happened, they fell out of the higher dimension.

In reference to the Garden of Eden, which served as Adam and Eve's earthly habitation, we can picture how things were in the beginning. I imagine with some surety, that fruit trees, all types of life, streams, rivers, gold, diamonds and all kinds of minerals and precious stones were in the garden. There was a continuity between everything that God created. We have evidence that animals could speak, whether audibly or telepathically, I don't know but I do have my opinion. The Bible indicates that the serpent walked upright and spoke to Eve, and she understood what it was saying. That means there was communication in the garden between God's creation and man.

# In the perfect world that God created, we see Adam and Eve operating by the technologies of God.

The Bible says that God walked with them in the cool of the day. When Adam and Eve fell, God began to look for them. Now get this: were they not all in the garden when God said, "Adam, where are you? Where are you?" He was in essence saying, "I cannot find you in the dimension where I created you to dwell. Where are you?" God came out, walking in the cool of the day and He was saying, "I'm looking for my voice; I'm looking for my image. I'm looking for the man that I created."

Adam had fallen out of the supernatural dimension. Thus, a portal had to be provided as a vehicle by which Adam could be restored. It was necessary for God to make an opening into the heavenly dimension, which would serve as a way for Adam to come back into alignment. The Bible says that God killed an animal to shed its blood. Why? Because the blood of the animal became a portal through which man could return to God.

Well, Dr. Nesbitt, what are you saying? I'm saying that God instituted the protocol wherein blood would speak on behalf of people, to appease the anger of God, providing justice and grace for humanity. Why? Because Adam lost authority over this world when he fell to a lower dimension. When Adam fell, he transferred rulership of the earthly dimension to Lucifer. This spiritual transaction, which took place by Adam's sin, gave Lucifer the lease on the earthly dimension until later, when Jesus redeemed all creation through the work of the cross.

For this reason, we must contend to be restored back to our rightful place. That is why we must pray. That is why we must find portals to access heavenly dimensions. A psalmist wrote a song about us going back to the Garden of Eden. And yes, we are. That said, we must find doors and gates that will serve as access points while we are yet living in our earthly bodies.

# The creator's original intent was for man to always operate in his superior God-like authority. Man was never intended to exist in a fallen state.

It has always been the Father's intention that man would have unfettered access to Himself and to His Kingdom, that man might rule, reign, subdue, be fruitful and multiply in the earthly dimension.

## Concept 4
*Kingdom technologies are essential to fulfill destiny*

We must come to terms with the fact that it is necessary to operate in such spiritual technologies as prayer, the Blood of Jesus, fasting, praise, worship, and the study of the Word to remain connected to God and ultimately fulfill His purposes in the Earth. Beside these, which most modern-day believers are familiar with, there are other technologies that are foundational to God's way of doing things. One in particular, which is fundamental to the Hebraic roots of our faith, is the observing of the appointed times that are on the <u>Hebrew calendar</u>. This book, "*Accessing Ancient Portals*," directs its readers to seriously consider this underutilized technology as a means of establishing God's timetable in our lives and aligning more perfectly with Him. As your thinking expands to embrace a greater scope of God's Word, you will naturally open Ancient Portals that will break curses, end demonic cycles, and more. Technologies are about to be revealed to you, dating back to creation and the exodus of the Jews from Egypt. They will provide deliverance from evil in many areas of life, including health, wealth, relationships and prosperity. By their very nature, these technologies give access to perpetual cycles of blessings. And, most importantly, understanding this technology will open to you a higher realm of revelation that will take you to a place of passionate intimate relationship with the Father, the Son, and Holy Spirit. Once this mystery is opened to you, your life will never be the same. Hallelujah!

For the record, I'm not speaking of man-made concepts, but rather mandates that were instituted by God Himself. These Ancient Portals, of which I speak cannot be accessed by any means other than by the very Power of God.

Again, Ancient Portals, serve as doorways, windows, or gates into realms and dimensions, creating a point of access between the heavens and the Earth. When a portal is open, the realities of Heaven can manifest in the Earth.

# CHAPTER TWO

# FOREVER

> *For the Jews who do not believe that Jesus Christ is the Messiah, observing the appointed times is just a law. But for all who believe that Jesus Christ is the way, observing the appointed times is a key to supernatural revelation.*

S easons are marked by divine appointments. These appointments often take on the form of mentors, mentees, helpers, and gleaners. In the Biblical context, Ruth was an example of three of the four. She was the mentee of Naomi. Ruth came into Naomi's life as a daughter-in-law. Ruth's husband died amid a myriad of misfortunes in their family, leaving both Ruth and Naomi without a means of support. The two formed an inseparable bond; Naomi discipled Ruth as her spiritual mother. Ruth embraced the teachings she received and grew to love and honor

Naomi. In an effort to be of help to her mother-in-law, Ruth went out into the fields to glean the leftovers of the harvest. The result was a supernatural promotion for both Ruth and Naomi that took them from the welfare rolls to a position of abundance and wealth.

Like Naomi, I have had the privilege of serving as a mentor and leader to many who have submitted to the discipleship of the teachings of Christ that the Father has given me to share. In one such case, and unbeknownst to me, was a young lady who had tuned her ear to the teachings that Holy Spirit had given to me regarding why the Body of Christ should embrace their Hebraic roots. After a couple years, our paths crossed. When we were introduced, there was an excitement in her voice. "I'm so honored to meet you," she declared with an over-the-top type of exuberance. I'd been experiencing an uptick in my schedule; all the while I was spearheading some projects and managing the normal day-to-day responsibilities I have as a pastor. Needless to say, there were a number of things vying for my attention at the time. I was polite, but of a few words. Honestly, my curiosity was a little peaked. I thought, "there must be a purpose for this introduction." After the brief conversation, we agreed that we would speak again soon.

In the fullness of time, I learned some things about this young lady. She was excited because of the feeling of peace that she felt in relation to the ministry that God has entrusted me with. In the past, she often had feelings of mistrust as she had been searching many years for a place to call home in the Kingdom. A few years before, she had quietly and unassumingly hung her hat on the post of Dominion World Outreach Ministries, the church that God led me to establish in Marion, Arkansas in the year 2002. She had been searching for an evangelistic ministry that was motivated by the desire to see the Kingdom come to pass in the lives of people. She found what she was looking for at Dominion. During our conversations she had much to say.

*"I like the fact that you are sensitive to the season that we are in," she said.*

*"The Father is faithful to give His people the means to perceive the times and seasons that's for sure," I responded.*

*"The fact that your ministry is keen on activating the special technologies of the Spirit needed to fulfill the call of God on this generation is so exciting to me!," she exclaimed.*

*"All Glory to the Father," I responded. "We are indeed on the cusp of the end of the age. Not only must we be prepared, but NOW is the time to execute the plans and strategies that have been communicated to us by His Spirit! That is why it is so important to transition onto His timetable. We, as Kingdom citizens, must clearly comprehend His revelation for the Body of Christ and become passionate about operating in the supernatural technologies that He has given us. By doing so we are guaranteed to be overcomers."*

This young lady went on to tell me how she believed that our conversation was ordained by Holy Spirit; she began to give her testimony.

She had been in a perpetual season of unrest for virtually all her life. No matter how hard she worked it was never enough. She said she never understood that toil was a curse and that the "curse of toil" had been broken by the shed Blood of Jesus Christ. At the time she began her quest for deliverance, she was middle-aged. The fact that she was getting older motivated her to seek out a way to put a stop to the endless cycles of hardship that she was experiencing.

Honestly, I was interested in knowing what had led her to observe the appointed times. This revelation is somewhat novel to the Western church. I figured there was a story behind her decision to do so. So, I asked her.

She told me that she had discovered teachings regarding the feast days, and what really captured her attention was the concept of the Moedim.

"In Leviticus 23, there are two different Hebrew words that translate "feast." The first word is "Mo-ahd," and is often translated "appointed time." Mo-ahd means to set an appointment, as in a set time or season, for a specific assembly or festival. The plural form of "mo-ahd" is "moedim." This particular word for feast refers to the weekly Sabbaths and all the Levitical Holy Days." [3]

The concept of the Moedim, as taken from Exodus 23:14, is where God tells the Israelites that the feast of Passover, Pentecost and Tabernacles are His appointed times. These are the times that He has set aside for His people to meet with Him. In Leviticus 23 God says, "these are my Feasts." He commanded His people to celebrate them **"forever."** What was so striking to her was the word "forever." The teachings on the feasts made it clear that the Feasts of God are not the feasts of the Jews, but they belong to God. In the King James version of the Bible, they are referred to as the "Feasts of the Lord." When she began to think about the mainstream holidays, she said she started to feel sick to the stomach. She started to reflect on the pagan origins of those Holidays, and how she had fervently celebrated them all her life. She said, "I felt physically ill, but I wasn't sure why. I just knew that there was something wrong." The words "celebrate my feasts forever" resonated in her heart. She knew that she had to line up with the Word of God.

The second thing that really stood out to her were the blessings attached to observing the feasts. There are seven feasts in all. She admitted that she dismissed four of the feasts, opting to only celebrate the three "primary" feasts for several years. As she came to understand that ALL seven feasts are a shadow of Jesus Christ the Messiah, she realized the importance of these celebrations. She said, "I felt like observing each celebration was a way of staying ready at all times for Christ's return." She didn't know that there was more in store for her than being ready for His return, as if that wasn't enough. After all, eternal salvation is everything right? But, out of the generosity of God's goodness, He began to pour out so many blessings.

The continuous cycles of hardship disappeared. In her own words, "life didn't feel hard anymore." She said she used to be anxious all the time. She felt like working extremely hard was a badge of honor and that being thankful for having barely enough to survive was a virtue. Sadly, this type of thinking could not have been further from the truth. The strongholds in her mind were reinforcing a covenant with an evil spirit that had brought about the "curse of toil" in her life. Thankfully, the shed Blood of Jesus Christ has made a way for every curse to be broken. When she realigned with the appointed times of God, supernatural portals of blessings opened in her life. This realignment caused the miracle of rest and the Shalom of God to manifest. Today, she is living a life of prosperity; what used to be difficult now comes with ease. With every opportunity to observe the appointed times in obedience to the command of God, her blessings continue to multiply more and more.

## Forever

## "These are the feasts of the LORD, even holy convocations, which ye shall proclaim in their seasons."
### LEVITICUS 23:4

As stated earlier, one of the key elements that resonated with the young lady in her account of why she chose to observe the appointed times was the word "forever." Forever is FOREVER! The fact that the Word of God states that the Lords feasts are referenced as HIS feasts and not the feasts of the Jews opened a portal of understanding that was further illuminated by the word Forever.

## The feasts are "His feasts" to be observed "forever."

These words should be enough to motivate every believer to come into a greater obedience unto God by observing His feasts. If nothing else, we should be asking the question, "Why are the feasts (the appointed times) so important to God?"

Note: The Word of God is also a portal. It is a portal of understanding that takes us to various dimensions of knowledge and wisdom in God. The feasts demand that we search out their meaning through God's Word, which is one of the many ways that blessings are opened up to those who observe His appointed times.

## The Appointed Times

In Hebrew moedim is a plural Hebrew word meaning "appointments" or "appointed times". Leviticus 23 contains significant references to God's appointed times. This word is sometimes translated as "holidays" or "festivals" but is better understood as divinely commanded appointments. Strong's Concordance #4150. Pronounced MO eh DEEM. Plural "moedim".[4]

Ezekiel 45 references the appointed times as "the feasts, the new moons, and the Sabbaths." Annual, monthly, and weekly observances are all considered Sabbaths (Shabbat celebrations) because they have one requirement....REST!. Note: Some observances are reverenced more highly than others by the Jewish people but all represent an opportunity to remember Elohim (God).

## Feasts, The New Moons, The Weekly Sabbaths

Feast days are celebrations where God's people remember Him for His mighty acts, His provision, and His protection. It is a joyful time when His people meet with Him. New moons/Rosh Chodesh (used interchangeably) are also a time when God's people would take time out to worship Him and to bless the upcoming month. The weekly Sabbaths put an emphasis on bodily rest taking time to meditate on God. Under the old covenant these special times were a part of the law.

## We have a better covenant

The people were required to adhere to these laws or suffer judgment. Today, we have a "much better covenant" according to Hebrews 8:6. Jesus is the fulfillment of the law, thus we are redeemed from the curse of the law and made righteous through Him. Yes, New Testament believers in the Bible observed the feasts and Sabbaths. Through Jesus, we have been restored to a personal relationship with God. We now observe His ordinances out of love for Him and not out of compulsion by the law.

> [16] Therefore do not let anyone judge you by what you eat or drink, or with regard to a religious festival, a New Moon celebration or a Sabbath day;
> [17] These are a shadow of the things that were to come; the reality, however, is found in Christ.
> [18] Do not let anyone who delights in false humility and the worship of angels disqualify you. Such a person also goes into great detail about what they have seen; they are puffed up with idle notions by their unspiritual mind.
> [19] They have lost connection with the head, from whom the whole body, supported and held together by its ligaments and sinews, grows as God causes it to grow.
>
> COLOSSIANS 2:16-19

## God judges the self-righteous

When people put themselves above others by self-righteous deeds this makes God very angry. Jesus called such people vipers!

> [23] Woe unto you, scribes and Pharisees, hypocrites! for ye pay tithe of mint and anise and cummin, and have omitted the weightier

matters of the law, judgment, mercy, and faith: these ought ye to have done, and not to leave the other undone.

[24] Ye blind guides, which strain at a gnat, and swallow a camel.

[25] Woe unto you, scribes and Pharisees, hypocrites! for ye make clean the outside of the cup and of the platter, but within they are full of extortion and excess.

[26] Thou blind Pharisee, cleanse first that which is within the cup and platter, that the outside of them may be clean also.

[27] Woe unto you, scribes and Pharisees, hypocrites! for ye are like unto whited sepulchres, which indeed appear beautiful outward, but are within full of dead men's bones, and of all uncleanness.

[28] Even so ye also outwardly appear righteous unto men, but within ye are full of hypocrisy and iniquity.

MATTHEW 23:23-28

Here, Jesus pummels the scribes and Pharisees with the bold-faced truth of who they really were, "hypocrites!" He reveals that it is necessary to first cleanse "that which is within the cup" (the heart), that the "outside… may be clean also." We can comprehend from these scriptures that Jesus is revealing a mystery as it relates to the soulish realm and the natural realm. The instruction here is to purify the soul (the internal parts) in order to achieve right standing (true righteousness and alignment) with God, thus bringing about an outward manifestation of God's glory. As we discuss Accessing Ancient Portals, understand that, for the believer, Ancient Portals are opened by accepting Jesus into our hearts and obeying His Word.

The scribes and Pharisees aligned themselves with the father of lies. They were deceived by their own pride and self-righteousness. Yes, they experienced selfish gain, but to their ultimate destruction.

*Ye serpents, ye generation of vipers, how can ye escape the damnation of hell?* MATTHEW 23:33

We cannot achieve true righteousness by works, only by accepting Jesus Christ as our Savior. Let us be sure to keep at the forefront of our hearts and minds that:

## Jesus Christ (Yeshua HaMashiach) is THE DOOR; He is the Way, the Truth, and the Life. No man comes to the Father (into alignment/oneness with the Father) except by Him.

Jesus is THE DOOR that gives us continuous unfettered access to The Father, the Kingdom, the Power of His Spirit (Ruach Hakodesh) and everything that pertains to Him. He is all in all. We don't follow His ordinances because we are bound by laws; we do so out of the freedom to do so, which comes through His salvation.

Regarding the topic at hand, the moedim are commandments/opportunities that God has provided us, which serve as a way to align ourselves with the frequency of Heaven and His blessings. They are special times on God's calendar when He calls us to meet with Him. As we take the opportunity to exercise this Kingdom principle of observing God's appointed times, we know that by doing so we are in all actuality observing Jesus Christ. Furthermore, I believe very strongly that observing the appointed times is a direct segue into the supernatural. These are the last days. The anti-Christ spirit has ramped up its agenda to decimate humanity. But, as we embrace the supernatural, we will see that not only will we survive, but we will thrive as we await Jesus' return.

## Weekly Sabbaths

The very first commandment that the Israelites received after the exodus from Egypt, even before the Ten Commandments were given, was "remember the Sabbath day." It is a sign between God and His people and a reminder of how He had delivered them from their oppressor. Observing the weekly Sabbath as a day of rest is also a reminder to us that we have been delivered from being slaves to sin by the shed Blood of Jesus Christ.

In addition, weekly Shabbats are in alignment with the cycle of seven, which is a supernatural technology that is linked to creation, symbolizing completion in both the spirit and natural world.

## Monthly Sabbaths

Rosh Chodesh or The New Moon means the beginning of the month or literally the "head of the month." It is the first day of every month in the Hebrew calendar, marked by the birth of a new moon. This is not a major feast, but still, it brings with it much symbolism. In short and like the weekly sabbath (Shabbat celebration), it is an opportunity for a supernatural reset. Monthly Shabbat's have a supernatural essence to them as they align with the new moon, which speaks to new opportunities, the passing away of the old, and regeneration.

*Seven Feasts*

There are seven feasts, all of which are types and shadows of Jesus Christ. The following are the lists and symbolic meanings of each.

## 1. FEAST OF PASSOVER
*Leviticus 23:4-8*

HEBREW NAME "PESACH". The Feast of Passover speaks of the crucifixion of Jesus Christ. Jesus Christ is our Passover Lamb. By Him we have escaped death and righteousness has been imputed unto us, for while we were yet sinners Christ died for us.

## 2. FEAST OF UNLEAVENED BREAD
*Leviticus 23:6*

Leaven represents sin. This moed points to Jesus' sinless life and how our sins were buried with Him. Note: Unleavened bread and wine are major elements of this feast. This speaks to the act of taking communion under the New Covenant. To us, this represents redemption through the broken body and shed blood of our sinless savior Jesus Christ.

## 3. FEAST OF FIRST FRUITS
*Leviticus 23:10*

First Fruits is celebrated on the third day after the sacrifice of the Passover Lamb. Jesus rose 3 days after His crucifixion. This moed points to Jesus' resurrection, and that he is the first of all brethren to rise from the dead.

## 4. PENTECOST (FEAST OF WEEKS)
*Leviticus 23:16*

HEBREW NAME "SHAVOUT". Pentecost points to the birth of the church of Jesus Christ and the giving of the Gift of His Holy Spirit.

## 5.    FEAST OF TRUMPETS          *Leviticus 23:24*

HEBREW NAME "ROSH HASHANAH". The feast of Trumpets points to the fact that Jesus will return at the sound of the trumpet.

## 6.    DAY OF ATONEMENT          *Lev. 16, 23:26-32*

HEBREW NAME "YOM KIPPUR". This moed points to sanctification cleansing through the Blood of Jesus Christ that is necessary to be prepared for Judgment Day.

## 7.    FEAST OF TABERNACLES (BOOTHS) *Lev. 23:34*

This moed prophetically points to the Millennial Reign of Jesus Christ here on Earth.

In the following chapters we will explore how the Ancient Portals are accessed, the specific blessings associated with the moedim, and how the cycles are activated by observing the moedim.

# CHAPTER THREE

# WHY HELL DESIRES TO CHANGE THE TIMES

*For it is not possible to be an active participant in the execution of a strategy if one does not know the plan.*

**W**hy did God institute a divine calendar? To better understand the reason for divinely appointed times, it is good to note that God is strategic. He demands organization and systems. When Adam and Eve were created, God instructed them to dress and keep the garden and to name the animals. Dress means to beautify and keep means to manage. Man has been doing this ever since. When you look around you can see innumerable systems used to classify all manner of creatures, places and things. For example, Taxonomy is the system used to classify plants, animals and microorganisms. This is the nature of God. He made man to find fulfillment in work. Thus, He gave man the elements to achieve happiness through creativity and productivity. One of God's primary purposes behind strategically placing man in the Earth was to expand His Kingdom. It was necessary for man to have the authority to function as God's representative to fulfill God's vision. The authority was transferred to satan. Ultimately chaos ensued, precipitating the flood that destroyed everything and everyone that was not in the Ark with Noah.

When Jesus came, He was given the redemption blueprint and was mandated to restore creation back to God and to give stewardship back to God's children. Jesus came through the lineage of the Hebrew people as they were the people who had been entrusted with the instructions on how humanity should operate in life. They are the keepers of the Torah. The literal meaning of the word Torah is "direction or instruction." From the moment Adam fell, God had a redemption map. As we reflect, we can see that His plan looks something like this: God put a reflection of Himself in the Earth and called it Adam and Eve. After Adam and Eve lost their authority to satan, Moses was given the Word of God. The Word then became flesh in the form of Jesus Christ, through whom the world was reconciled. Upon reconciliation, man received God's Spirit, The Holy Ghost, to live inside of Him. Upon receiving the Spirit of God, man received the power to become the Sons of God giving man Godlike attributes. John 1:1-5 says:

In the beginning was the Word, and the Word was with God, and the Word was God. The same was in the beginning with God. All things were made by him; and without him was not anything made that was made. In him was life; and the life was the light of men. And the light shineth in darkness; and the darkness comprehended it not.

Why did He give man special powers? He gave us power to be His sons by opening the well of salvation to us, but He went further, causing that well to overflow that others might be saved also. Acts 1:8 states:

But ye shall receive power, after that the Holy Ghost is come upon you: and ye shall be witnesses unto me both in Jerusalem, and in all Judaea, and in Samaria, and unto the uttermost part of the earth.

These were Jesus' last words to His disciples right before His ascension. The purpose behind the strategic element of filling believers with His Spirit was to create an army of powerful witnesses. The older Saints would say, 'He will give you power to talk right, power to walk right, and power to live right.' They were correct; yet there is a higher dimension that exists in this revelation. He has given us the power to do all the things that Jesus did, including heal the sick, raise the dead, perform all kinds of miracles, and to preach the Gospel to others so that they can be translated from darkness to light. Bless the name of Jehovah the Most High! Are you following the plan? This is God's victory strategy mapped out from Adam (God's image) to Moses (God's Word) to Jesus (the Word made flesh) to us believers (God's dwelling place). And, when our work is done, He will receive us unto Himself according to Acts 1:9-12.

> And when he had spoken these things, while they beheld, he was taken up; and a cloud received him out of their sight. And while they looked steadfastly toward heaven as he went up, behold, two men stood by them in white apparel; Which also said, Ye men of Galilee, why stand ye gazing up into heaven? this same Jesus, which is taken up from you into heaven, shall so come in like manner as ye have seen him go into heaven. Then returned they unto Jerusalem from the mount called Olivet, which is from Jerusalem a sabbath day's journey.

And, when He receives us up into heaven, the entire Body of Christ will have been purged and perfected. One thing I do know is that He desires a Bride that is pure, who has been tried by fire and come forth as pure gold, and whose garments are pure white.

Feel free to go back and read this paragraph one more time, because it is revelatory to the point that each time you read it a fresh Anointing will come upon you to see God as the Master Architect that He is.

The point of this chapter so far is that God is strategic. I could give many more examples of the strategic nature of God, but the point has been made. He is all knowing; it is He who holds the cards of destiny in His hands. There is no evil, no devil, no power that can compare to Him. It is not possible for God to be opposed by any formidable opponent – for there are none! The wickedness you see today will soon be no more. When you see the many things that are coming to pass, Jesus said, "See that you not be afraid." DO NOT BE TERRIFIED. Why? Because it's all in the plan.

## God gives His children revelation

The key to a successful plan is knowing the plan. God says, "In all thy getting, get understanding." Solomon said, "An intelligent heart acquires knowledge, and the ear of the wise seeks knowledge." It is not possible to be an active participant in the execution of a strategy if one does not know the plan. God does not reveal everything all at once. Even Jesus spoke in parables because it is not given to the world to understand the mysteries of the Kingdom. But, in due season, He gives the precious pearls of understanding to His children. I believe that now is the time for God's children to come into spiritual alignment in preparation for His return. These are the perilous times which the Bible warned us of. Psalm 11 says:

> ¹ In the LORD put I my trust: how say ye to my soul, Flee as a bird to your mountain?
> ² For, lo, the wicked bend their bow, they make ready their arrow upon the string, that they may privily shoot at the upright in heart.
> ³ **If the foundations be destroyed, what can the righteous do?**
> ⁴ The LORD is in his holy temple, the LORD's throne is in heaven: his eyes behold, his eyelids try, the children of men.
> ⁵ The LORD trieth the righteous: but the wicked and him that loveth violence his soul hateth.
> ⁶ Upon the wicked he shall rain snares, fire and brimstone, and an horrible tempest: this shall be the portion of their cup.
> ⁷ For the righteous LORD loveth righteousness; his countenance doth behold the upright.

Let us highlight verse 3, "If the foundations be destroyed, what can the righteous do?" There are some fundamental elements of God's strategy to redeem humanity. One is to separate the righteous from the unrighteous through sanctification. Another is to endow the righteous with wisdom, knowledge and understanding. Once these are accomplished, it is His expectation that the Righteous will become active participants in the fulfillment of His plan. The motivation for His plans are rooted in His love for His children; our willing participation in His plans must be out of our love for Him! Where the scribes, Pharisees, and Sadducees missed it was that they possessed knowledge, but did not possess love. Today, we have a better covenant through the Blood of Jesus Christ. Psalm 11 states that "His countenance doth behold the upright." In other words, His eyes are on the Righteous. We have His attention, and He is ensuring our victory by the technologies of the Kingdom that He is working in and through us.

Right now, the wells of revelation are being re-dug as it relates to the foundations of our Faith. God commissioned me to bring a greater understanding regarding the supernatural technologies that are inherent to our Hebraic roots which Jewish people employ to their benefit. Jewish people have not only an awareness of times, seasons, the Hebrew alphabet and vibrational frequencies associated with speaking Hebrew words, they also have extreme veneration of the Torah.

**Def.: Torah**

noun

1.  Instruction, doctrine, law
2.  (in Judaism) the law of God as revealed to Moses and recorded in the first five books of the Hebrew Scriptures (the Pentateuch).

The Torah is the compilation of the first five books of the Hebrew Bible, namely the books of Genesis, Exodus, Leviticus, Numbers and Deuteronomy. In that sense, Torah means the same as Pentateuch or the Five Books of Moses. It is also known in the Jewish tradition as the Written Torah.

The Torah and the Old Testament at-large are the record of the foundations that are spoken of in Psalm 11:3. These foundations are the map that leads to The Door, which is the revelation of Jesus Christ. Within the Old Testament are hidden keys that unlock these revelations. The "Master Key" is the mystery of the moedim, which gives a clear picture of the times and seasons and what the Body of Christ must do. Satan knows that if the bride remains asleep, she will not be prepared. He knows that if God's people are faithful to meet with Him during the appointed times, Our Father will give us divine downloads including: instructions, direction, supernatural impartations, and blessings. Satan, hell's angels, and the entire kingdom of darkness have come down in fury, "because he knows that his time is short." I am convinced that Elohim has chosen this time to reveal the mystery of the moedim (appointed times) because understanding the supernatural nature of God's blessing cycles (divine appointments) are key to our preparation for His soon return.

*What do the moedim reveal?*

# God has a plan, and He is revealing the mystery of the moed to us because He wants us to know what to do!

*Signs and seasons*

According to I Chronicles 12:32, the children of Issachar were men that understood the times to know what Israel ought to do. Some believe that it means that they were very gifted in discerning current events in a way that gave them a clear advantage. Some scholars believe this means that they understood astronomy and physical science. I believe that they had an understanding of astronomy and physical science, and this is why. They were blessed to receive the most fertile portion of the promised land. They were also known as the donkeys (hardest workers) of the 12 tribes and are noted for being among the richest of the tribes. When the tribes went to battle, the tribe of Judah, who understood the technology of praise and worship went first. The tribe of Issachar, who understood the times and seasons and how to discern what to do went second. Then the tribe of Zebulun, who understood the principles of commerce and finance went third.

**This is a spiritual strategic principle; the powers of PRAISE, UNDERSTANDING (discernment), and ECONOMICS work together to bring about supernatural results.**

"Tradition says, "Issachar became a farmer and God prospered his efforts 10,000-fold."[5] Their success in the development of their land tells me that they understood astronomy in order to know the best time to sow their seed and what seed to sow at that time. It also tells me that they understood astronomy in a way to understand what God was speaking to His people. For example, the three wise men, who some believe may have been of the tribe of Issachar, followed the star to find Jesus. The sons of Issachar discerned that it was time for David to be King. They also supported Deborah the judge, which led to an important military victory for Israel. Could it be that they knew these things by observing and recognizing the symbols and signs associated with the appointed times?

As a contemporary example, it is notable to acknowledge the customs of today's Jewish people. Often, they will defer to go to court, make business deals or act on important matters until after Rosh Hashanah (the head of the year). Many of them, including those who are none practicing Jews for most of the year, will give their largest offerings and make their most significant contributions to the poor during that time. They believe that they will have better outcomes after honoring God at this appointed time.

Rosh Chodesh, head of the new month, is also a strategic time for the Jewish people. During this time, they take note of the heavens and of God's mighty works to discern how to move forward. Now, this is not an excuse to condone astrology. To the contrary, astrology is the belief that the position and movements of celestial bodies dictate what happens in a person's life. This is pure wickedness! When the children of Israel were preparing to go over into the promised land, God warned them saying, "beware lest you raise your eyes to heaven, and when you see the sun and the moon and the stars, all the host of heaven, you be drawn away and bow down to them and serve them" (Genesis 4:19). Astrologers are listed among magicians and enchanters; God forbids such practices. On the other hand, Genesis 1:14 says, And God said, Let there be lights in the firmament of the heaven to divide the day from the night; and let them be for signs, and for seasons, and for days, and years. If we look at this scripture more closely, we see that God says that the sun, moon, and stars, which are the lights in the firmament, are for "signs." The word sign in Hebrew is the word "avah" (Strongs #H184), which means to sign, mark, or describe with a mark; to extend or mark out; to point out. Thus, it is apparent that God uses the heavens to convey messages. The heavens do not dictate the affairs of man, but rather God is the one who controls our lives. He holds the destiny of the entire world in His hands. Rather, He allows us to hear His instructions through His creation and in many revelations associated with the appointed times. I'm of the opinion that we should see God in everything.

## When the People of God are mindful to observe His signs and seasons, they too can gain the advantage of insight that the sons of Issachar had.

During Rosh Chodesh (the head of the month) we are reminded that He speaks through signs and to take into account His mighty acts. For example, the sign of the month of Iyar, which occurs between April and May on the Gregorian calendar, is the ox eating grass, which reminds us that He will satisfy us through His abundant provision. Also, it was during the month of

Iyar that the bitter water was turned sweet for the children Israel while they were in the desert, and the month that Jesus ascended to heaven. If we take a moment to observe this moed (appointed time) we would be reminded that Our Father promises to take that which was meant for evil and turn it too good. We would also be reminded that, like Jesus, we are ascending to higher realms and dimensions in Him by faith while we are in our mortal bodies and after that we will ascend to be with Him. This is just an example.

There are 12 months; they all have numerous symbols attached to them. Let's look at the month of Tishrei. It has more than six points of symbolism attached to it.

| | |
|---|---|
| HEBREW MONTH | Tishrei |
| GREGORIAN CALENDAR | September/October |
| TRIBE | Ephraim |
| STONE | Jacinth |
| CONSTELLATION | Libra |
| ALPHABET | Lamed |
| SENSE | Touch |
| ORGAN | Gallbladder |

The symbolism attached to each month point to the nature, the purposes, and the plans of God and the work of His dear son, Jesus Christ. In the case of Tishrei, its association with Ephraim can represent double fruitfulness. When Ephraim, who was the grandson of Jacob, is studied, it can be concluded that those who know and do the will of the Father, will be fruitful.

What is the first thing we must do to get into the will of the Father? We must accept His son, Jesus Christ. This Ephraim analogy has been given to clarify what I mean by "symbols are attached to each month." A list of symbols has been provided in the resources section located at the end of this book.

Rosh Chodesh is a minor Sabbath, but the feasts and weekly Sabbaths are moeds that carry more weight for the Jewish people. In chapter two, we covered how the feasts reveal the work of Jesus Christ. The weekly Sabbaths remind us to enter into His rest and that He is our source. Abba Father has given us a divine calendar of His appointed times for a reason.

1.  He has a plan.
2.  He wants to reveal His plan to His children.
3.  The Hebrew calendar gives us the advantage, like the Sons of Issachar who knew the times and seasons and knew what to do.

# Satan Does Not Want You to Have the Map

Satan knows that the children of God already possess the victor's crown; his goal is to trick us into giving our victory to him. This is the reason HE LIES. He lied to trick the angels into rebelling against God in heaven. He lied to trick Adam and Eve into giving him their authority. He is still lying today. As a matter of fact, he is telling the same old lies. He told Eve "you can be like God." Well, she was already like God because she was made in His image.

This is the lie that is driving some of the most wicked ideologies of today. He is telling people, "you will be like God," "you can live forever." These are the deceptions, along with greed, that are behind some technological advancement, particularly in the medical field. Technologies have become so advanced that the memories of one person can be transferred to another body or even into machines. Genetic modification is so advanced that the attributes of a child can be selected before being born. This is just the tip of the iceberg in terms of what is already being done, not even considering how quickly technology will advance in the near future.

That is not the subject at hand, but it does give insight into the personality of our arch enemy. He recreates himself as Pharoah and Goliath in a million different ways. He is the slave master, just as Pharaoh was, enslaving people to sin. He amplifies his voice to make himself look bigger than he is. Like Goliath, fear is one of his primary tactics. The truth is that satan's main power is the power to deceive. This is why he tries to paint untrue pictures of God. He knows that God is beautiful and very attractive to humanity; after all, we have our origins in Him. He knows that if we see the truth of God, we will believe in Jesus and be reconciled back to the Father. He knows that if we receive the infilling of the Spirit of God we will walk in true Power!

This is the reason that all of hell is raging against the Revelation of Jesus Christ in any and every form. Daniel, speaking of the beast, which is of the spirit of anti-Christ, said that "he shall speak great words against the most High, and shall wear out the saints of the most High, and think to change times and laws." The New Living Translation says it this way:

> He will defy the Most High and oppress the holy people of the Most High. He will try to change their sacred festivals and laws, and they will be placed under his control for a time, times, and half a time.
>
> DANIEL 7:25 (NLT)

Satan has changed the times and laws to deceive the Body of Christ. Since the times of Constantine until now, the papacy and its predecessors have issued universal edicts that have deceived the entire world into abandoning the commandments of Elohim and submitting to the gods of this world. This has been achieved by merging paganism and Christianity. The times of the moedim that God commanded His people to observe "forever" have been altered or abandoned in favor of various alternatives. Many of the holidays that people all over the world have become accustomed to celebrating include: Advent, All Saints' Day, All Souls' Day, Ash Wednesday, Autumn Equinox, Carnival, Christ the King Sunday, Christmas, Easter, Epiphany, Fat Tuesday, Good Friday, Halloween, Harvest Parties, Holy Saturday, Holy Thursday, Lent, Mardi Gras, Marian Feast Days, Maundy Thursday, May Day, New Year Celebrations, Spring Equinox, St. Patrick's Day, Summer Solstice, Trinity Sunday/Sabbath, Valentine's Day, and Winter Solstice. As we review this list of widely observed celebrations it is obvious that the profane has been mixed with the holy. Satan seeks to mimic Elohim through his counterfeit strategies. A number of these holidays are even listed on the satanic calendar and are observed by satanists as their high holy days. Some of these holidays open major portals to death and hell. This is one of the primary reasons many people are possessed and oppressed by demons, experience perpetual failure and hardships, and suffer under the impact of various curses.

By changing the times and seasons, satan has sought to advance his own purposes.

1. He desires to cause believers to worship him (satan) through pagan holidays that are designed to replace the moedim (appointed times);

2. He wants believers to walk in disobedience by distracting them from remembering the mighty acts of God.

3. His seeks to divert believers away from the cycles of blessings, which include: prosperity, wealth, divine downloads, and perpetual open heavens that come by keeping God's feasts.

These objectives have been achieved and are continuing to drive the Church deeper and deeper into a state of apostasy, meaning to abandon one's faith. Jesus warned that the end will not come before there is a great falling away. Based on the description of apostasy, I would dare to say that the great falling away has already happened to some degree. It is now incumbent upon true ministers of the Gospel to prepare the remnant to stand. I decree that even while you are reading this book, the Spirit of Revelation is coming upon you to help you to stand in Power and in Glory, fulfilling the purposes and plans of the Father for your life.

Know this! Understanding the mysteries revealed by the appointed times is indeed the map that serves to light the way of believers as the world devolves into a state of gross darkness. The observance of the moedim opens portals of perpetual blessing, which arm the Saints against satan's agenda and keeps believers from falling for satan's tricks. Understanding and observing the appointed times is literally THE KEY that opens the heavens perpetually! The divine calendar of Elohim unlocks the doors to:

- perpetual rest and regeneration in mind, body and spirit;
- perpetual restoration in the natural and spiritual dimensions;
- the seven blessings for those who observe His feasts in accordance with Exodus 23; and
- understanding of the times by way of the celestial signs, the revelations of Jesus Christ revealed through the Sabbaths and the Feasts.

Sadly, satan's strategies have been relatively effective. I would assume that is why the New Testament refers to the Saints as "The Remnant" (a small remaining quantity of people). This is the day of deception; the masses are being led to hell in droves. But, Jesus said, "be of good cheer for he has overcome the world." When Jesus said this, He was speaking to the 11 disciples. He knew that they would see and experience challenging situations. He wanted them to understand that the battle had been won for them. Sure enough, after Jesus' departure, the Apostle's ministries exploded with many great works such as healings, casting out demons, imparting the Holy Spirit, resurrection of the dead, working of miracles, mass conversions, being translated from one place to another including into spiritual realms, experiencing divine visions and dreams, etc.

Why were the Apostles so powerful? It was because they were the first to walk in the upgrade from the Old Covenant to the New Covenant through the revelation of Jesus Christ. In other words, they were the first to keep the law in context with the revelation of Jesus Christ. Yes, they kept the Sabbaths and the Feasts, giving their offerings and doing good deeds (mitzvah's) such as healing the sick and making provision for widows and orphans.

**Def.: mitzvah**

noun

1.  A commandment of Jewish law

2.  In common usage, a mitzvah often means "a good deed"

What brought about a significant difference for the disciples was that they did not keep the law out of a spirit of obligation, but rather with the revelation of Jesus Christ, understanding who He was. In doing so, they walked in the fullness of God's blessings and power. Abba Father is calling us to do the same today! When we keep the Sabbath, as Jesus and the Apostles did, we are keeping Jesus Christ because he is our eternal Sabbath. When we keep the feasts, as Jesus and the Apostles did, we are keeping Jesus. All of the feasts are merely depictions that clearly reveal who He is. We do these things as a way of finding intimacy with the Father through His dear Son.

The powers of darkness know that God has a strategic plan for His bride. That plan has been laid out in the form of a map, which is revealed through the Biblical feasts on the Hebrew calendar. When we choose to observe these appointed times, we are in essence keeping an appointment with God who will meet us at that time. This alignment with God opens the heavens and causes us to experience the instruction, direction, and blessings of Our Loving Father. Satan's goal is to disrupt our alignment with God and to cause the Saints and the world to bow to him instead.

Right now, your heart is most likely feeling inspired by a strong desire to come into greater alignment with God through greater obedience. Just begin to thank Him and know that He has already given you the power to come into agreement with Him with ease. As you do, your life will surely change for the better.

### 1 JOHN 5 AMP

[1]Everyone who believes (with a deep, abiding trust in the fact) that Jesus is the Christ (the Messiah, the Anointed) is born of God (that is, reborn from above—spiritually transformed, renewed, and set apart for His purpose), and everyone who loves the Father also loves (a)the child born of Him.

[2] By this we know (without any doubt) that we love the children of God: (expressing that love) when we love God and obey His commandments.

[3] **For the (true) love of God is this: that we habitually keep His commandments and remain focused on His precepts. And His commandments and His precepts are not difficult (to obey).**

[4] For (b)everyone born of God is victorious and overcomes the world; and this is the victory that has conquered and overcome the world—our (continuing, persistent) faith (in Jesus the Son of God).

The true love of God is this: that we habitually keep His commandments and remain focused on His precepts. And His commandments and His precepts are not difficult to obey.

# CHAPTER FOUR

# HINDS FEET FOR HIGH PLACES

> *Find delight in Adonai –*
> *And He will cause you to ride on the*
> *heights of the land.*

I n Chapter Two, I began by saying that "seasons are marked by divine appointments." I was speaking of a divine appointment between myself and a person God had placed in my path. As I reflect on that statement, I realize that seasons in our lives and in the Body of Christ as a whole are even more so marked by divine appointments with Abba Father.

## There is always a portal open when we come into the presence of God.

The scriptures say, "in His presence is the fullness of joy and at His right hand are pleasures forever more." This is the nature of God to bring joy, blessings, increase, multiplication, wisdom, protection, comfort, ease, love, and every good thing imaginable. When we align with times, places, people, or things that pertain to God, it is likely that we will connect to a portal. In His presence or by connecting with elements that are linked to God, we experience dimensions in Him. It's like traveling into higher dimensions where there are no limitations of space or time.

I remember the movie, Back to the Future, that was released in the 1980's. The storyline was that of a young man (Michael J. Foxx) who was able to travel back and forth through time in what we now understand to be a portal. We are trained to think of time in our three-dimensional reality when, in truth, we exist in a multi-dimensional world where the past, present, and future are all taking place at the same time. This is why Jesus' sacrifice can atone for your sins—past, present, and future. He himself became a portal through which we can access all the benefits of being sons and daughters of God. Remember, a portal is defined as a "gateway", "door", "opening", "entry point" or "entry way" into another realm or dimension. It is a segway between the Earth and the heavens. It's a place of supernatural activity where God and the angels can legally interact in the affairs of man.

We often hear the cliché, "God is in control," but that is not totally accurate. Psalm 115:16 says, "the highest heavens belong to the Lord, but the earth He has given to mankind." As the Alpha and Omega, the Beginning and the End, He is in control. However, in terms of the Earth, He gains control through permission from man or by opening portals. Portals are of the utmost importance because he who controls the portals controls everything connected to it. As we expand our understanding of portals, it is important to also know that portals can be found "in" or "attached to" people, places, things, spaces in time, and to specific purposes.

## Portals Attached to People

Let's look at some examples of people in the scriptures who had portals attached to them.

### Enoch

Even though there are only six scriptures in the King James Version of the Bible relating to Enoch's impact on the Earth—the six reveal some powerful truths related to portals. It appears that Enoch was not close to God before the age of 65. It was after the birth of Methuselah that he cultivated a personal relationship with the Lord. His faithful and consistent walk with the Lord created a portal that ultimately allowed him to physically transcend Earth's atmosphere. He was here, then he was gone.

We then find him mentioned again as one who, during those 365 years of life on Earth, prophesied the return of the Lord. This prophecy ref-
*JUDE V14*
erenced in the book of Jude actually comes from the Book of Enoch. Jude's reference to the Book of Enoch validates that the early church considered Enoch a part of the sacred scriptures.

In Enoch 37:4-9, Enoch prophesied how the Lord would return and how He would use portals and windows. Enoch's ability to see this far in the spirit is proof that he himself was a portal.

And first comes forth the great luminary called the sun; and his circuit is like the circuit of the heavens, and he is entirely filled with flaming and heating fire. The wagons on which he ascends are driven by the wind, and the sun descending disappears from the heavens and returns through the north in order to reach the east, and is led that he comes to that portal and shines on the surface of heaven. And thus he comes forth, in the first month, in the great portal, and he comes forth from the fourth of these six portals toward the east. And in that fourth portal, from which the sun comes forth in the first month, there are twelve window openings, from which a flame proceeds when they are opened in their time. When the sun rises from the heavens he comes out of that fourth portal thirty mornings, and descends directly into the fourth western portal of heaven. And in those days the day is daily lengthened, and the nights nightly shortened to the thirtieth morning.

This excerpt from the Book of Enoch is fascinating because it gives powerful insight into the revelation of portals and how they function.

## Elijah

The second example of a person who had a portal attached to their life is the Prophet Elijah. II Kings 2:11 states, *And it came to pass, as they still went on, and talked, that, behold, there appeared a chariot of fire, and horses of fire, and separated them both asunder; and Elijah went up by a whirlwind into heaven.* Elijah, a man of strong prayer and consecration, had a portal connected to his life. The Bible records that he was able to open and close the heavens at will. He closed the heavens so that there was no rain for three years. During the drought resources became scarce, yet the ravens miraculously fed Elijah by the Brook of Cherith. Through Elijah, a poor starving widow experienced supernatural increase, multiplying her oil and meal. He opened the portal of unlimited provision that sustained her and her son until the drought was over. It was this same widow whose son died and was brought back to life at the cry of Elijah (I Kings 17:1-24; James 5:17).

His exodus from the earth was like that of Enoch. He was and then he was no more, for he was caught up in a whirlwind. His spirit, soul, and body were taken away in a portal.

## Jesus

Jesus is our primary model of how oneness with God brings about open Heavens. *Jesus saith unto him, I am the way, the truth and the life; no man cometh unto the Father, but through me (John 14:6).* There are many scriptures that prove that Jesus Himself was a portal. His confession of being the only way to access the Father demonstrates this truth. In addition, you see an active operation between heaven and earth everywhere He went.

He went from turning water into wine to being resurrected from the dead. The Books of Matthew, Mark, Luke and John together record approximately 36 miracles that Jesus performed, but John notes in John 21:25 that the miracles of Jesus were too numerous to record. He said, *if everyone should be written, I suppose that even the world itself could not contain the books that should be written.* This is proof that Jesus was the door to the Father. After the resurrection, Jesus left Earth by ascending into Heaven.

# Interestingly, Enoch, Elijah, and Jesus all left Earth through a type of ascension (taking up/taking away).

This is an indication that they operated under an open heaven where there was a perpetual portal opened between them and God, and that portal was connected to their lives. They are examples of how alignment (oneness) with God through a life of consecration and purpose allows a person to consistently operate above the natural plane.

## Portals Attached to Places

Like people, portals can be attached to places. The following are some examples.

### Bethel was a portal

> When Jacob awoke from his sleep, he thought, "Surely the Lord is in this place, and I was not aware of it." He was afraid and said, "How awesome is this place! This is none other than the house of God; this is the gate of heaven."
> - GENESIS 28:16-17 (NIV)

The Lord told Abraham to leave his family and go to a place that He would show him. Abraham made a stop at an area originally known as Luz. Genesis 12:8 says this was the area where Abraham encountered God. It was there that Abraham built an altar to the Lord. This is the same place where

Jacob has an encounter with God. There, Jacob saw angels ascending and descending on a staircase that went from heaven to Earth with God standing at the top of it. Jacob changes the name of the area from Luz to Bethel which means "house of God" or "house of Bread" in the Hebrew language. This was a portal for accessing the presence of God. We can tell this was a sacred place because of what happened to King Jeroboam. 1 Kings 12:28-30 records, King Jeroboam created two golden calves, put one in Bethel and forced the people to worship it. God's response for violating the sacred space was to destroy the King and his entire lineage from the face of the Earth according to 1 Kings 14:8-11.

## The Wilderness was a portal

> Yet he gave a command to the skies above and opened the doors of the heavens; he rained down manna for the people to eat, he gave them the grain of heaven. Human beings ate the bread of angels; he sent them all the food they could eat.
>
> - PSALM 78:23-25 (NIV)

Here we observe how God opened a portal that supernaturally supplied the children of Israel with food while on their exodus from Egypt. Imagine a door opening in the heavens and raining down "angel food" every day for forty years. Now we can clearly see how the millions of people that were traveling through the wilderness never got sick (Psalm 105:37). They were living in a supernatural dimension, eating supernatural food every day! And if "you are what you eat," then they literally became supernatural and didn't even know it.

## *The Isle of Patmos was a portal*

> After this I looked, and there before me was a door standing open
> in heaven. And the voice I had first heard speaking to me like a
> trumpet said, "Come up here, and I will show you what must take
> place after this." At once I was in the Spirit, and there before me
> was a throne in heaven with someone sitting on it.
> - REVELATION 4:1-2 (NIV)

Here, the Apostle John, who was banished to the island of Patmos, is invited
to come up to heaven by Jesus. We know that the remaining chapters in the
book of Revelation describe what John saw when he accessed this portal.

## *Jerusalem is a portal*

> After he said this, he was taken up before their very eyes, and a
> cloud hid him from their sight. They were looking intently up into
> the sky as he was going, when suddenly two men dressed in white
> stood beside them. "Men of Galilee," they said, "why do you stand
> here looking into the sky? This same Jesus, who has been taken
> from you into heaven, will come back in the same way you have
> seen him go into heaven." Then the apostles returned to Jerusalem
> from the hill called the Mount of Olives, a Sabbath day's walk from
> the city.
> - ACTS 1:9-12 (NIV)

The City of Jerusalem is a modern-day example of an active portal in the
Earth. This portal was used at the point of Jesus' ascension into heaven, and
it will be the same portal that will be used when He returns to Earth. This is

the underlying reason why the kingdom of darkness fights so hard for that small piece of real estate known as Israel. The enemy thinks if he can control the gates of that portal that he may have a chance at restricting Jesus' return. It is incumbent upon us as believers to pray for the peace of Jerusalem so that we may prosper (Psalm 122:6).

Take note of certain supernatural phenomena that occur in specific places. Some cities have certain characteristics that could indicate that a portal is open. Portals can be open for a short period of time, open and close at specific times, or can remain open continuously. Raise your awareness so that you can be as the sons of Issachar who knew what to do.

# Portals Attached to Things

*The brass serpent was a portal*

> And the Lord sent fiery serpents among the people, and they bit the people; and much people of Israel died. Therefore the people came to Moses, and said, We have sinned, for we have spoken against the LORD, and against thee; pray unto the LORD, that he take away the serpents from us. And Moses prayed for the people. And the LORD said unto Moses, Make thee a fiery serpent, and set it upon a pole: and it shall come to pass, that every one that is bitten, when he looketh upon it, shall live. And Moses made a serpent of brass, and put it upon a pole, and it came to pass, that if a serpent had bitten any man, when he beheld the serpent of brass, he lived.
>
> - NUMBERS 21:6-9

When we look at the people of Israel in Numbers 21, we see that the posture of their soulish realm led them to not only speak against God and Moses, but also to refuse to have faith in God for their provision. Ultimately, they stepped out of the supernatural dimension that sustained their earthly life in the wilderness. As a result, sickness and death came upon them. Therefore, a portal had to be recreated to restore the children of Israel's access to the dimension of supernatural provision. In this case, the brass serpent became a portal for restoration and healing, patterned after the typology of Jesus Christ. Jesus bore our sickness and was made sin for us to bring us back into right relationship with God. He was lifted up on the cross so that whoever believes on him would have eternal life. Likewise, the brass serpent was lifted up so that the people of Israel could, by faith, be healed and restored (John 3:14-15; Matthew 8:17; II Corinthians 5:21).

## Samson's hair was a portal

> So he told her everything. "No razor has ever been used on my head," he said, "because I have been a Nazirite dedicated to God from my mother's womb. If my head were shaved, my strength would leave me, and I would become as weak as any other man.
> - JUDGES 16:17

Samson was a man who operated in the miraculous; he was able to do mighty exploits when the Holy Spirit came upon him (Judges 14:5-6,19; 15:14; 16:28-30). The Philistines were Israel's enemies, and Samson was their protector. The Philistines sought through Delilah an opportunity to overpower and restrain Samson. After numerous attempts by Delilah to learn Samson's secret, we see here that Samson, in error, revealed to her the portal to his strength, which was his hair. Samson's hair was the portal whereby he accessed The Kingdom of Heaven and was infused with divine strength from the Holy Spirit to defeat armies; these feats would have been impossible to accomplish in his own humanity. The moment Samson confided in Delilah, an agent of the devil, Samson stepped out of alignment with the Kingdom of God and into alignment with the kingdom of darkness. He became vulnerable to a satanic attack when his hair was cut. This immediately made him weak because the portal was closed, and the Lord departed from him. It was only after his hair grew back that he was once again able to access the heavens and perform his last mighty act that would help to deliver Israel from the oppression of the Philistines for many years.

## *The Ark of the Covenant was a portal*

> So David would not remove the Ark of the Lord unto him into the city of David: but David carried it aside into the house of Obededom the Gittite. And the Ark of the Lord continued in the house of Obededom the Gittite three months: and the Lord blessed Obededom, and all his household. And it was told king David, saying, The Lord hath blessed the house of Obededom, and all that pertaineth unto him, because of the Ark of God. So David went and brought up the Ark of God from the house of Obededom into the city of David with gladness.
>
> - II SAMUEL 6:10-12

The Ark of the Covenant was a portal directly into the presence of the Lord. Elohim gave a specific protocol that the Ark was to be transported on the poles by the priests so that they would not touch it and die (Numbers 4:15, 7:9; Exodus 25:12-15; Deuteronomy 10:8; Joshua 3:8-14). This protocol was not adhered to when a new cart was used to bring the Ark of the covenant to Jerusalem from the house of Abinadab where it had been for many years. While transporting the Ark, they arrived at Nacon's threshing floor. Uzzah, a driver of the cart, tried to stabilize the Ark with his hand in an effort to keep it from falling. He was struck by God and died after touching the Ark. You see, the Kingdom of God is governed by protocols and operates according to instructions and laws. Obedience is required in everything that pertains to the Lord and the carrying out of every part of His will. Because Uzzah mishandled the portal of the presence of God, death was the result. However, once the Ark was relocated to the house of Obededom, a Levite, God began to bless Obededom and everything attached to his household. This is because the portal—the Ark of the Covenant—rested on Obededom's estate, and because He was mindful to follow the protocols set by God. Therefore, God's holy presence could abide once again, and the supernatural realm of blessings could be experienced.

## The hem of Jesus' garment was a portal

> In the crowd that day there was a woman who for twelve years had been afflicted with hemorrhages. She had spent every penny she had on doctors but not one had been able to help her. She slipped

in from behind and touched the edge of Jesus' robe. At that very moment her hemorrhaging stopped. Jesus said, "Who touched me?" When no one stepped forward, Peter said, "But Master, we've got crowds of people on our hands. Dozens have touched you." Jesus insisted, "Someone touched me. I felt power discharging from me."

- LUKE 8:43-46 (MSG)

At the edge of Jesus' garment was a fringe, which consisted of a tassel with a blue cord. This tassel was representative of heaven and healing (Mark 6:56; Luke 8:44; Numbers 15:38-40), thereby making it a portal where people could access a spiritual dimension of healing from heaven. Now, when the woman who was hemorrhaging approached Jesus and touched the fringe of His garment, she said within herself, "I shall be made whole" (Matthew 9:21). She shifted her belief system from one based on faith in man to faith in God. She went from spending all her finances on doctors to putting her trust in Jesus to heal her. Consequently, as a result of her faith in God, which is the currency of heaven, she was able to make an exchange for her permanent healing through the portal of Jesus' garment. This divine flow of exchange between Heaven and Earth is the reason Jesus felt power go out from Him.

## Paul's handkerchief was a portal

God did extraordinary miracles through Paul, so that even handkerchiefs and aprons that had touched him were taken to the sick, and their illnesses were cured and the evil spirits left them.

- ACTS 19:11-12 (NIV)

Paul was a man of great faith who operated in the fullness of the spirit. In this passage of scripture, we see that God is performing special and unusual miracles through Paul in Ephesus. These miracles were unusual because of how God brought them about. You see, everything in the Kingdom of God and in the realm of the spirit must be accessed. In this instance, the handkerchief becomes the access point or portal into the realm of the spirit whereby the miracles of Heaven could be manifested in the Earth. Ultimately, the miracles that were wrought allowed the Word of the Lord to be magnified so that the works of the devil in this region were destroyed. Many put away their idolatrous ways and embraced the Gospel of Christ.

## Portals Activated by Speech

*Solomon reminds us the words we speak are portals*

> Death and life are in the power of the tongue, and those who love it shall eat the fruit thereof.
>
> - PROVERBS 18:21

Solomon, deemed the wisest man to live, had much to say about the mouth, tongue, and lips. They all are key components of speech. This aligns perfectly with Mark 11:23 that says, "*You can have what you say.*" If you want to live and enjoy life you must take advantage of the portal of speech. Believers and unbelievers both use their mouths to make transactions between Heaven and Earth.

The words that we speak carry frequencies and vibrations that open and close doors and gates in the spirit realm. The "*worlds were framed by the*

*Word of God"* (Hebrews 11:3). Man is made in the image and likeness of God, and like Him our words bring the realities of the spirit into the natural.

In addition, music also carries frequencies that open portals. This is why praise and worship are so effective in accessing other dimensions. The Word says that God *inhabits the praises of His people* (Psalm 22:3).

# Time Sensitive Portals

*Some portals are attached to seasons*

> For an angel went down at a certain season into the pool, and troubled the water; whosoever then first after troubling the water stepped in was made whole of whatsoever disease he had.
>
> - JOHN 5:4

Here we find that at a certain time of year, a portal for healing opened at the pool of Bethesda. The community residents knew that the portal existed and the time of year it could be accessed. Many of the sick, diseased, and infirmed would gather in hopes of exchanging their malady for God's divine healing.

# Portals That Open at the Appointed Times/ Moedim

*The appointed times are portals*

> Three times in a year shall all thy males appear before the LORD thy God in the place which he shall choose; in the feast of unleavened bread, and in the feast of weeks and in the feast of tabernacles; and they shall not appear before the LORD empty.
> - DEUTERONOMY 16:16

There is no better description of a portal than what the Lord implemented when He chose specified times for His people to meet with Him during His appointed feasts throughout the year. Since He is the one who has called for these special times to meet with His people, He is faithful to show up. In other words, when His people are obedient to His command, portals are guaranteed to open. HalleluYah!!!

# Portals that Open for a Specific Purpose

*Salvation*

> An angel from the Lord spoke to Philip, "At noon, take the road that leads from Jerusalem to Gaza." (This is a desert road.) So he did. Meanwhile, an Ethiopian man was on his way home from Jerusalem, where he had come to worship. He was a eunuch and an official responsible for the entire treasury of Candace. (Candace is the title given to the Ethiopian queen.) He was reading the prophet

Isaiah while sitting in his carriage. The Spirit told Philip, "Approach this carriage and stay with it." Running up to the carriage, Philip heard the man reading the prophet Isaiah. He asked, "Do you really understand what you are reading?" The man replied, "Without someone to guide me, how could I?" Then he invited Philip to climb up and sit with him. This was the passage of scripture he was reading: **Like a sheep he was led to the slaughter and like a lamb before its shearer is silent so he didn't open his mouth. In his humiliation justice was taken away from him. Who can tell the story of his descendants because his life was taken from the earth?** The eunuch asked Philip, "Tell me, about whom does the prophet say this? Is he talking about himself or someone else?" Starting with that passage, Philip proclaimed the good news about Jesus to him. As they went down the road, they came to some water. The eunuch said, "Look! Water! What would keep me from being baptized?" He ordered that the carriage halt. Both Philip and the eunuch went down to the water, where Philip baptized him. When they came up out of the water, the Lord's Spirit suddenly took Philip away. The eunuch never saw him again but went on his way rejoicing. Philip found himself in Azotus. He traveled through that area, preaching the good news in all the cities until he reached Caesarea.

- ACTS 8:26-40 CEB

The evangelist, Philip, who had a passion for the work of the Kingdom has a divine encounter with an Angel who instructs him to take a certain route when traveling from Jerusalem to Gaza. Following the instructions, he meets an Ethiopian Eunuch, who was over the treasury department for Queen Candace. During this encounter, he introduces the Eunuch to the

Gospel message of Jesus and baptizes him in water. When they come out of the water, Philip disappears and is never seen again by the Eunuch. Philip is immediately transported to Azotus; the Eunuch is still on the riverbank. The portal opened because Philip's assignment was complete with the Eunuch, and he was transported in the spirit 25 miles away to do evangelistic work in all the cities from Azotus leading to Caesarea.

Notice here that more than one portal opens for the fulfillment of Philips mission: 1) the Angel appears, 2) the Gospel message opens the portal of salvation, 3) Baptism opens a portal of blessing in the Eunuch's life for a renewed life in Christ, and 4) Philip completes his assignment and a portal opens, translating him from his current location to another. Portals open continuously in the life of believers who walk in the ways of God.

## Portals Attached to Dispensations

When Pentecost Day arrived, they were all together in one place. Suddenly a sound from heaven like the howling of a fierce wind filled the entire house where they were sitting. They saw what seemed to be individual flames of fire alighting on each one of them. They were all filled with the Holy Spirit and began to speak in other languages as the Spirit enabled them to speak.

- ACTS 2:1-4 (CEB)

There have been many messages expounding on the giving of Holy Spirit as recorded in Acts 2. Through these messages we have been taught about His purpose, personhood, gifts, and language. It is a great privilege to have Him both active and operative in our lives, but what I would like to highlight here, specifically, is His entrance into the earth realm. His entrance was no typical entrance! The sudden sound and presence that filled the entire house where the 120 expectant believers were sitting was the entrance of the Holy Spirit through a portal open in the heavens that manifested tangibly in the Earth.

This portal brought forth Holy Spirit and thrust the Kingdom into a Church Age, as this was the time that the Church as we know it was born. With the Church Age came the dispensation of Grace. We see here that God opens portals during major shifts in times. These shifts can be defined as dispensations.

## Believers are Made to Dwell in High Places

This chapter has provided a whirlwind of impartation, as you have been prompted to reflect on fascinating accounts of open portals and the various means by which they were opened or accessed.

In each case what we see, is in essence, "an ascension" above the natural. Even in cases where the Power fell, the response was going up. For instance, in the upper room their tongues went up in flames of Holy Ghost Fire! Philip was transported away from where he was. Those who were healed transcended sickness to the higher place of healing. The Ark brought about a higher level of prosperity. And on and on. This brings me to the point made in Psalm 18:33.

## He maketh my feet like hinds' feet, and setteth me upon my high places.

A hind is a female deer that is renowned for her surefootedness. Her home is in the mountains, where she successfully climbs to heights. The bride of Christ is like that.

We are designed to scale the highest places. We are called to break boundaries. Now that we are aware of the unlimited technologies that are available through faith in our Lord Jesus Christ, we can now transcend earthly realms and dimensions, and live on a higher plane in Christ.

Portals are literally all around us. Accessing them begins with a life of faithful obedience to our Heavenly Father. God has commanded us to enter His provision through the Appointed times wherein we are called to worship Him. He has also given the Gift of Holy Spirit to dwell in us. We can ask for ears to hear and eyes to see opportunities to receive downloads from Heaven, whether it be healing, wisdom, joy or any other manifestation of God; it does not matter. Let your faith soar, raise your expectation, and purposefully come into alignment with Abba Father through Jesus Christ.

## CHAPTER FIVE

# OUR BLOODLINE BLESSING

*Like the biological sons of Abraham,*
*Isaac and Ishmael, the blessing extends*
*to us as well.*

The "cycle of blessings" God uses to prosper His people has a circular pattern that is never ending unless there is something that breaks the cycle. It is hidden in His Word and clearly articulated through His calendar (the Hebrew calendar), which is why thinking from a Hebrew standpoint allows us to gain a greater revelation of Him. It is believed that Hebrew is the language of Angels[6] and the Hebrew alphabet, specifically His name own name YHWH, was used to frame the worlds!

> Through faith we understand that the worlds were framed by
> the word of God, so that things which are seen were not made of
> things which do appear.
> - HEBREWS 11:3

Though I have not codified this belief, I would say that this is probable. Scientists say that YHWH can be found in the sequences of man's DNA. [7]Some even purport to have identified God at the atomic level of all matter. The thoughts of God can change the molecular structure of things. He merely speaks, and miracles happen. Even the intentions of His thoughts act as seeds of manifestation. His thoughts are His will, the engine by which everything happens. For this reason, thinking from a Hebrew mindset can change your life. Our Hebraic roots are a path that take us back to the origins of our existence in God. They give us a clear picture of who we are in Him.

Again, *If the foundations are destroyed, What can the righteous do?* (Psalm 11:3) If we as believers do not have a grasp on our foundations, how will we stand in the last days? I believe this is why the ancient technologies of the Faith are being revealed to the Body of Christ. By God's divine timing, these things are being revealed for the sole purpose of fortifying the Church in preparation for His return. And, make no mistake about it, He is coming for a glorious church!

It is also worth noting that heavenly revelations are not the only revelations being released to mankind in these end times. All technologies are being made clearer – evil and light. As the Bible prophesied, mankind is becoming more wicked and more wise and knowledge is increasing exponentially.

The revelations of the Kingdom are for such a time as this. Mankind is not wise enough to discern the mind of God, but through God's systems, which are revealed by understanding our Hebraic roots, believers can have a clearer picture of the times and seasons of God.

To help you see what it means to think and understand from a Hebrew mindset, let's look at the life of Jews in different sectors of society.

## The Jewish people; our example

Jewish people are disproportionately wealthy compared to other ethnicities. Jews make up only 0.19% of the world's population. That is less than 2 tenths of a percent. Yet, out of the 50 richest people in the world, approximately 25% are Jewish. Moreover, 35% of the "2015 Forbes 400" (which require one's wealth to be at least $1.1 Billion) are Jewish. Among them are Larry Ellison, the wealthiest Jew in the world who is the founder of the tech giant Oracle Corporation. His net worth is $116.3 billion. Another is Michael Bloomberg, the 20th wealthiest person overall and former New York City Mayor. His net worth is $59 billion. Yet another is Mark Zuckerberg, one of the world's youngest billionaires at age 30. His net worth is $130.8 billion.

To make the connection between the Jewish mindset and financial success, I will use Larry Ellison as an example. Larry Ellison was born to a 19-year-old single Jewish Mother named Florence Spellman. At 9 months old, Larry became ill with pneumonia. At that point, his mother Florence determined that she was not capable of caring for him and asked that he be placed with her aunt and uncle, Louis and Linda Ellison. "Ellison was raised in a religious household and often attended synagogue."[8] Despite the fact that he was raised in a Jewish home, Larry is not a religious person. It is reported that he is a great supporter of Israel and loves the country very much. So, what could have caused portals for financial blessing to overtake Mr. Larry Ellison, who is the richest man in the (Forbes) world at the time of this publication?

1.   He may have had the blessing of the first born.
2.   His bloodline, including his uncle and aunt, observed the Sabbath and the Feast Days.
3.   He was raised Jewish so he most assuredly received the priestly blessing given to boys.

In context, we can glean the following understanding: the blessing of the first born is a double portion anointing. The first-born son in the Jewish culture receives a double portion for their inheritance because they are expected to be the caretakers of their parents in their old age. Larry was likely the first-born son; I surmised this from the sparse details that I could find when researching his life. The blessing of the first born is not just about an inheritance, it is a spiritual mantle. You may notice that the first born usually is the one in the family that has a knack for business and is the one who prospers the most, or at least shows the greatest potential, in the way of finances. Secondly, Larry was raised as a practicing Jew. This means that they observed the high holy days. There are at least seven blessings attached with the observance of these appointed times in accordance to Exodus 23.

The Word of God says that He shows love to a thousand generations to those who love Him and keep His commandments. This means that there are bloodline blessings that are perpetual. My final observation is that he almost definitely received the priestly blessing given to Jewish boys. Today, this blessing is spoken over the children each Friday evening when the Sabbath/Shabbat begins.

Numbers 6:22-26 is the scripture where the Priestly Blessing can be found.

> The Lord said to Moses, 'Tell Aaron and his sons, this is how you are to bless the Israelites. Say to them: "The Lord bless you and keep you; the Lord make his face shine on you and be gracious to you; the Lord turn his face toward you and give you peace."

The proclamation spoken over the boys before the primary blessing says the following:

יְשִׂמְךָ אֱלֹהִים כְּאֶפְרַיִם וְכִמְנַשֶּׁה.

*Yesimcha Elohim k'Ephraim v'chi-Menashe.*
*May God make you like Ephraim and Manasseh.*

The words spoken over the girls say:

יְשִׂמֵךְ אֱלֹהִים כְּשָׂרָה רִבְקָה רָחֵל וְלֵאָה.

*Yesimech Elohim k'Sarah Rivka Rachel v'Leah*
*May God make you like Sarah, Rebecca, Rachel and Leah.*

After these pronouncements are made the Priestly blessing is spoken over them, which says:

יְבָרֶכְךָ יְהוָה וְיִשְׁמְרֶךָ.

יָאֵר יְהוָה פָּנָיו אֵלֶיךָ וִיחֻנֶּךָּ.

יִשָּׂא יְהוָה פָּנָיו אֵלֶיךָ וְיָשֵׂם לְךָ שָׁלוֹם.

*Yivarechecha Adonai v'yishmerecha*
*Ya'er Adonai panav eilecha vichuneka*
*Yisa Adonai panav eilecha v'yasem lecha shalom*

*May God bless you and keep you.*
*May God shine His face on you and be gracious to you.*
*May God turn His face toward you and grant you peace.*

The name Ephraim (pronounced Eph-ra-yim) in Hebrew means "fruitful and prosperous." The name Manasseh (pronounced Me-na-she) in Hebrew means "God has made me forget my hardship." As you can see, embracing the Hebraic foundations of the faith has a powerful impact.

Let us also consider the impact of the Hebraic mindset in the areas of education, literature and media. In the United States, Jewish people make up only 2.6% of the population yet between 9% and 33% of students in leading universities in the U.S.A are Jewish. Those Jewish students are: 13 times more likely to study law, 6 times more likely to study sociology, 10.4 times more likely to study economics, 9.6 times more likely to study physics, 8.9 times more likely to study political science, and 7.4 times more likely to study mathematics. 33 % of Nobel Prize winners are Jewish. Major media networks such as ABC, CBS, NBC were founded and are run by Jewish people. Major news outlets owned and run by Jews include the New York Times, Washington Post, The Wall Street Journal, Time, Newsweek, U. S. News and World Report

You see, historically the Jewish people have been entrusted as the keepers of God's law. They have been chosen to serve as the template for how the rest of the world should honor God's systems. In following their good example, not the bad ones, we too can live in unending cycles of prosperity, which are clearly shown through the statistics above.

It is not a coincidence that while Jews make up 2% of the U.S. population and 0.19% of the world's population, they own much of the world's wealth. In times past, I would have said that these statistics exist solely because they are God's chosen people, but now I understand that there is so much more at work in the lifestyle of these people. They have tapped into a portal that has existed in scripture for thousands of years.

## Our bloodline blessing

When we think of the Hebraic mindset and our Hebraic roots, we reflect on the fact that Abraham is the father of faith. Abraham is considered the progenitor of three religions, Judaism, Islam, and Christianity. Judaism came through Isaac the son of promise and Christianity followed. Islam came through Ishmael the son who came out of an act of disobedience. Judaism was given the Torah (the laws and statutes of the faith) and Christianity was given the revelation of Jesus Christ and the Apostles doctrine. Even though Abraham submitted to the ill-founded suggestion of his wife Sarah and had a son by her handmaid Hagar, God still found fit to extend a blessing to Ishmael.

> And as for Ishmael, I have heard thee: Behold, I have blessed him, and will make him fruitful, and will multiply him exceedingly; twelve princes shall he beget, and I will make him a great nation.
> - GENESIS 17:20

Ishmael was the first born and he and his mother may have felt a sense of privilege that came with that status. The Bible says that Sarah, the wife of Abraham, "saw" Ishmael mocking during a feast that was being held for Isaac to celebrate his weaning. It is not clear what exactly Ishmael was doing, but it is clear that Sarah was triggered. In Genesis 21:10 Sarah said to Abraham,

## "Cast out this slave woman and her son; for the son of this slave woman shall not inherit along with my son, Isaac."

Abraham was distressed by everything that was going on because he loved Ishmael also. God spoke to Abraham and told him not to be upset and to listen to Sarah because his seed would be called through Isaac. But then God says, *AND ALSO of the son of the bond woman will I make a nation, because he is thy seed.*

So, Abraham puts them out to wander in the wilderness with a bottle of water on her back. When the water ran out, Hagar began to despair thinking that they were going to die. She lifted up her voice and began to cry. It was then that an Angel appeared and told her that God said He would make Ishmael a great nation. Water materialized in the desert and their lives were spared. The Arab people are the descendants of Ishmael. They are known for wealth, some of which has been derived from oil, natural gas, gold, silver and minerals. Saudi Arabia, an Arab country, holds half of the world's oil reserves. [9]

Despite that fact the Ishmael was dispossessed, he desired full rights as a son of Abraham. And because of the righteous judgment of God, he also received a blessing because he was Abraham's son.

I believe that it stands to reason that when messianic believers, those who believe that Jesus is the Messiah, reject their Hebraic heritage as the engrafted sons of Abraham, they are in fact rejecting a significant part of their inheritance. Like the biological sons of Abraham, Isaac and Ishmael, WE STILL GET A BLESSING TOO! We can also operate out of the supernatural economy of heaven and walk in dominion when we choose to embrace our Hebraic roots. It's time for believers to stand up, receive our inheritance, and take dominion!

# CHAPTER SIX

# THE HEBREW CALENDAR:
# HEBRAIC MINDSET

*There is a consistency and an empowerment that comes with unlocking the mysteries that are contained in our Hebraic roots...*

Thor here are some revelations that will help us to embrace our Hebraic roots. Understanding the Hebraic roots of our faith is also important to know because they hold keys that will allow us to tap into the supernatural benefits of observing the appointed times. This chapter gives revelation into the following: the Hebrew alphabet, the Name of God, and the Hebrew Language.

# Alphabet

## Original Hebrew/Paleo Hebrew Alphabet

Paleo Hebrew is the oldest form of Hebrew.

The Samaritans are, according to themselves, the descendants of the Northern Tribes of Israel that were not sent into Assyrian captivity and have continuously resided in the land of Israel. The Torah Scroll of the Samaritans use an alphabet that is very different from the one used on Jewish Torah Scrolls. According to the Samaritans themselves and Hebrew scholars, this alphabet is the original "Old Hebrew" alphabet, also called "Paleo-Hebrew.[10]

This form of the Hebrew alphabet is characterized by overtly recognizable depictions of various objects or animals. A numeric value is assigned to each letter[11].

## Modern Hebrew Alphabet

Ktav Ashuri (Hebrew: כְּתָב אַשּׁוּרִי, ktav ashuri "Assyrian script"; also Ashurit) is the traditional name of the Hebrew alphabet, used to write both Hebrew and Jewish Babylonian Aramaic. It is also sometimes called the "square script", the term is used to distinguish the *Ashuri* script from the Paleo-Hebrew script.

This form of the Hebrew alphabet is also associated with various objects or animals and the number that is assigned to it but is written in an updated styling influenced by the Hebrews' time in Babylonian captivity.

# His Name is YaHuWaH

God's name is Ya-Hu-Wa-H (YHWH), also written as YHVH and spoken as Yah, Je-Ho-Va-H, Ye-Ho-Va-H, and Ya-H-We-H. In Paleo Hebrew, the original Hebrew, there was no J sound or V sound. Even though the 6th letter in the Hebrew alphabet (vav) may have a "vha" sound to it based on contemporary dialects, the original sound would have been a (waw) "wha" sound. Thus, some scholars have concluded that the original pronunciation of YHWH's (YHVH) name is Ya-Hu-Wa-H.

## Warning

As we are meditating on the name of YHWH, we must address His name with honor and awe for He is the Most High Elohim. Exodus 20:7 says, *Thou shalt not take the name of YHWH thy Elohim in vain; for YHWH will not hold him guiltless that taketh his name in vain.* It is one of only two of the Ten Commandments that have a curse immediately associated with them for those who break it. I would also like to assert that I personally am grieved by the trends that are clearly blasphemous towards His name which is often used in comedy, acting and expletive words. When I see and hear these things, Holy Spirit signals my emotions to let me know that He is not pleased. Those of you who are spiritually minded have likely felt the same type of sadness, grief, or even vexation. WARNING: Do not participate in these activities! Do not even find enjoyment in them. For, according to Romans 1:32, those who do such unrighteousness are worthy of death. Do not even speak the name of YHWH if you do not have a reverential fear for

Him. But to those who know Him and earnestly call upon His name, there is a glorious reward for knowing, meditating on, and calling His name. Moses wrote a song referred to as the Song of Moses:

DEUTERONOMY 32 NKJV
Give ear, O heavens, and I will speak;
And hear, O earth, the words of my mouth.
Let my teaching drop as the rain,
My speech distill as the dew,
As raindrops on the tender herb,
And as showers on the grass.
For I proclaim the name of YHWH:
Ascribe greatness to our Elohim.
He is the Rock, His work is perfect;
For all His ways are justice,
El of truth and without injustice;
Righteous and upright is He.

## The benefits of knowing His name

In Deuteronomy 32:3 Moses declares, "I will publish the name of YHWH." The key to the preservation and glorification of the end time church is the publishing of His name! One of the reasons Jewish people have had a distinct advantage is because they know His name. His name is a key that unlocks portals. His name is a mystery that God has been trying to shed light on since the beginning. The Jewish people have, even back to the day of Elijah, made every effort to keep the name YHWH from being written, spoken or heard. Yet, all indications show that they, the Jewish people did not delete the name of YHWH from their sacred texts, even unto this day[12].

It is also understood that they speak the name of YHWH in private while assigning titles to Him in public such as El (the Ugaritic term for god that can refer to a pagan god, the God of Israel or the might of angels), Adonai (my sovereign/great Lord Master), Abba (of the Aramaic: Father I will obey You; Daddy; Pappa), Elohim (of the Hebrew: supreme one; all powerful one), Ha-Shem (of the Hebrew: the Name), etc. The name YHWH appears in ancient manuscripts over 7,000 times, yet His name is not mentioned once in our modern-day Bible, but rather has been replaced by the name "Lord." Some believe they hid it during Babylonian captivity because they believed the Babylonians would blaspheme His name. To keep His name holy, they concealed it. Of course, there may be other reasons as well, since the Jewish people have continued this practice until this very day.

YHWH desires for us to know His name according to the scriptures.

- Isaiah 52:6 says, "Therefore My people shall know My name."
- Exodus 9:16 says, "And for this reason I have raised you up, in order to show you My power, and in order to declare My Name in all the earth."
- He has promised not to forsake those who know His name according to Psalm 9:10, which states, "And they that know thy name will put their trust in thee: for thou, YHWH, hast not forsaken them that seek thee."
- Jesus released the mandate for the glorification of YHWH's name in John 12:28 that says, "Father, glorify Your name"
- YHWH is blessed when we call His name according to Psalm

105:1, "give thanks to YHWH, call on His name."

- YHWH is exalted when we use His name, according to Psalm 83:18 which says, "May people know that You, whose name is YHWH, You alone are the Most High over all the earth."

- Those who meditate on His name are written in the Book of Remembrance according to Malachi 3:16. "And a book of remembrance was written before him for those fearing Ya-Hu-Wa-H and for those meditating on His name."

- There is even a special protection to those who know His name. Psalm 91:14 says, "I will protect him because he knows my name."

I included this segment because, as the mystery of the Hebrew language is opened up to you, it is foundational for you to know the most important letters of all, Yod Hey Waw (Vav) Hey (YHWH). Intellectually, you learned a few key sounds in different dialects and some differences between Paleo Hebrew and modern Hebrew. But, by the power of the Spirit of Understanding a portal just opened to you that will give you direct access to ancient portals.

| | |
|---|---|
| The heavens hear | those who PUBLISH His name! |
| He protects those who | KNOW His name! |
| He will not forsake | those who CALL His name! |
| He is blessed by | those who GLORIFY His name! |
| He will be made known by | those who EXALT His name! |
| The Book of Remembrance holds the names of | those who MEDITATE on His name! |

According to Joel 2:32, *Everyone who calls on the name of YHWH will be saved.* Do you see how His name opens portals of blessing, protection, etc.?

Another intriguing revelation about YHWH's name is how His name is revealed in the names of His servants. One example is the name Elijah, which is Eliyah in Hebrew. It reveals the sound of YHWH's name through the Yah sound. There are approximately 140 Bible names that reveal YHWH through the name Yah, such as Uriah (Uriyah) and Zechariah (Zecharyah). Another revelation that gives insight into His name are examples that reveal the sound Yahu. The name Matthew, which is Matithyahu in Hebrew. It reveals the sound of Ya-Hu-Wa-H's as the Yahu sound. There are at least 70 such names in the Bible, such as Obadiah (Obadyahu), which means servant of Yah.

The greatest person to ever carry the name of Ya-Hu-Wa-H's name was His dear son, Jesus. In Hebrew, Jesus' real name is Joshua/Yehoshua (Yahushua). The name Yahushua was shortened reflecting influences during Babylonian captivity, but would have been pronounced Yahushua before that time. Yahushua reveals the Yahu sound of Ya-Hu-Wa-H's name and literally means, Yahuwah Saves!

YHWH has been ascribed many names of greatness. Among those are YHWH Sabaoth (the Lord of Hosts/Angel armies), YHWH Rapha (the Lord my Healer/Restorer). Scripture declares, the people who know their God will display strength and take action (Daniel 11:32). The sound of YHWH's many names releases a frequency that accomplishes incalculable shifts in multiple dimensions. It calls Angels to action, it activates Holy Spirit, it alerts Abba Father to pay attention to us, it activates the power of the Blood of Yahushua HaMachiach (Jesus the Christ/Messiah). It also activates faith in us causing us to submit to the leading of YHWH's Spirit. So, we will fight when we speak His name, Ya-Hu-Wa-H Sabaoth, because by the frequency that is in that name our spirit, soul, and body recognizes and becomes aware that He is the Lord of Angel Armies for that situation, and that we have an army of Angels fighting with and for us!

The revelation of these technologies is powerful and life changing. To him that has an ear let him hear what the Spirit is saying.

# Hebrew Language
## English compared to Hebrew

The English language is derived largely from Phoenician, Latin (the language of Rome), and Greek. It is a language of spell-binding words rooted in Masonry and other idolatrous beliefs. As is true with all languages, the spoken word "utterances" embody "source, energy, and force[13]. What that means is that words carry a frequency or a current. Due to the influence of Masons and others on the English language, English words may have associations that are outside of their immediate meaning. For example a relationship is not immediately associated with a ship that sails the seas. But when words with the suffix "ship," like "relationship" or "apprenticeship" are traced back to the origins of how the English language was constructed, one might find remote connections between the word with the suffix "ship" and maritime laws.

On the other hand, Hebrew is not a language of secret meanings, which are meant to deceive. Rather, revelations of the hidden meanings in the Hebrew language are dependent on a person's relationship with YHWH. YHWH desires for everyone to have a relationship with Him; thus, His ultimate goal is to reveal His mysteries to His children. His alphabet, His language, His Word, His Spirit, His revelations are all gifts to His children. When we crack the code of His alphabet, Earthly language, Word, or Heavenly language by the power of His Spirit we are then able to open portals that reconnect us to our divine nature in Him through Our Lord and Savior Yahushua Hamashiach/Jesus Christ.

In Hebrew, one word, as a rule, has a single meaning. Hebrew letters are expressed by symbols and each letter has a number assigned to it. By investigating the meanings of the symbols and the numeric code that is intrinsic to each number a deeper message can be assessed. Also, one may choose to take a Hebrew word for face value without much concern for any ungodly inferences. Words in the English language cannot be taken for face value but must be understood within a context because the majority of English words have multiple meanings. My research shows that this is not coincidental. It seems that the devil may be in the details, with the originators of the language creating a linguistic syntax that was meant to be understood and strategically used by the ruling class to keep commoners under subjection. On the other hand, there is evidence that Hebrew is indeed the original language of man. *According to the Biblical record of names, Adam and his descendants spoke Hebrew.*[14] In my opinion it stands to reason that Hebrew, having a pure syntax, would have a stronger vibrational essence. Simply stated, the Hebrew language is a Holy language given by YHWH, therefore the power of God Himself is resident within the letters and words of the Hebrew language.

To sum up the relevance of words, I would like you to understand that all words give off electromagnetic vibrations[15] Words have the power to heal and the power to harm. Words have the power to create and the power to destroy. *Through faith we understand that the worlds were framed by the word of YHWH, so that things which are seen were not made of things which do appear* (Hebrew 11:3). The English language is a bastardized language, meaning it is not original but is derived from different languages, has many meanings, and has secrets, and often wicked inferences that are not meant to be understood by the common person. Hebrew is YHWH's language and serves as a direct portal between God and man. It originates directly from YHWH and can be traced back to Adam. YHWH is one with His word according to John 1:1. YHWH esteems His word above His name according to Psalm 138:2. His Word is His communication (communion) with man. His Word expresses (brings to pass) His covenant promises to man. *In the beginning was the Word and the Word was with YHWH and the Word was YHWH* (John 1:1).

## The Believer's heritage

Jesus himself was the Word made flesh according to John 1:14. Hebrew is the only language that originates directly from YHWH. Although the Hebrew alphabet and language was given to the Hebrew people, it is still a direct and significant part of our heritage as believers, and I'll prove it. Romans 8:16-17 says, "The Spirit itself beareth witness with our spirit, that we are the children of YHWH: And if children, then heirs; heirs of YHWH, and joint-heirs with Christ." Christ was of the Hebrew heritage; though Aramaic may likely, but not certainly, have been His first language, He strongly embraced His Hebraic roots as evidenced by the research of scholar The Rev. Dr. Mark D. Roberts who states:

> There is one story in the Gospels that strongly suggests Yahushua knew and spoke Hebrew. In Luke 4, Jesus went to the synagogue in His hometown Nazareth. In the midst of the gathering, he read from the scroll of the prophet Isaiah. This reading was most certainly in Hebrew. Even though he (may have) spoke Aramaic as his first language, Jesus had learned Hebrew, like almost all Jewish men in his day.[16]

If Yahushua embraced His Hebraic roots and we are joint heirs with Him, then His heritage is now our heritage, and we possess all the rights and privileges of that heritage. Please note that the supernatural technology of the Hebrew language is not the only technology that opens ancient portals, giving us access to realms and dimensions in YHWH. But it, along with the Hebrew calendar, provides a systematic method, through Yahushua Hamashiach/Jesus Christ, by which we can operate on higher planes of existence. The key word here is systematic. By understanding the principles that you are being taught in this book, no longer must you wait 38 years by the pool of Bethesda for the stirring of the water. No longer must you wait on the priest to go in once a year to have your sins forgiven. And, you do not have to wait on an unction to be prepared for our soon coming King, because you will always be watching and ready! There is a consistency and an empowerment that comes with unlocking the mysteries that are contained in our Hebraic roots that brings about cycles of blessings, unlimited potential, and a greater supernatural capacity in Christ. I would also like to emphasize that the Hebrew calendar fosters a very consistent communion with YHWH through His Son and His Word and even continuous prophetic actions on a daily, weekly, and monthly basis, and during His feasts.

Also note, if you are reading this book and your native language is not English, merely place what has been said about the origins of words within the context of an example. Whether you speak Spanish, French, or Zulu, the message is the same. Hebrew is the official language of YHWH, but praise be unto His name, He can speak through any language! As a matter of fact, He can communicate through groanings that cannot be uttered according to Romans 8:26. AND, on the day of Pentecost He gave us His Spirit, which includes our heavenly language, which gives us the ability to use these technologies by the power of the Spirit of YHWH and not by our own strength. Do not worry about dotting every "i" and crossing every "t" to keep up with the law in a legalistic way. Rather, look at these revelations as opportunities for greater intimacy with Abba Father, and ask for His Grace to come into greater alignment with the things of YHWH.

Also note, as you continue to read this book, you will find that more Hebrew names such as Yahuah (God), YHWH (God), Yahushua HaMashiach (Jesus the Messiah), Ruach Hakodesh (the Holy Spirit) will be used to help orient you to their use.

# CHAPTER SEVEN

# THE HEBREW CALENDAR:
# THE MOEDIM

> *In scripture, YHWH set forth a*
> *foundational mandate to be observed*
> *by all believers, which is to celebrate His*
> *feasts.*

Technis chapter explains each of the appointed times and reveals their meaning in the context of the revelation of the Messiah (Jesus Christ) and suggestions on how we should celebrate them.

## Ancient Portals

The Hebrew calendar is made up of days, months, and years like the Gregorian Calendar. There are specific days on the Hebrew calendar that require YHWH's people to meet with Him. The special days are called moedim which is the plural of the word moed and means "appointed times." Each facet of the Hebrew calendar has a portal connected to it, which can be opened on a cyclical basis by those who understand and observe YHWH's special days.

## Hebrew vs. Gregorian calendar

The Hebrew calendar is a lunar based calendar that reveals the times and seasons based on the cycles of the moon. The Gregorian calendar is based on the cycles of the sun.

### Def.: gregorian

*adjective*

1. The calendar as reformed by Pope Gregory XIII. in 1582, including the method of adjusting the leap years so as to harmonize the civil year with the solar, and also the regulation of the time of Easter (a feast/festival/celebration to the goddess Ishtar/eostre) and the movable feasts (a holy day whose date is not fixed to a specific date) by means of epochs.

*noun*

2. One of a club or brotherhood somewhat similar to the Freemasons, which existed in England in the early part of the eighteenth century. *See Gormogon.*

The Word says that he, satan, would seek to change the times and the seasons. By merely considering the very definition of the word Gregorian, we can plainly see diabolical forces at work. That being said, we now have the awareness to know that when people synchronize their lives with the world's calendar, they are literally coming into alignment with the satanic Babylonian system! The book of Revelation warns us to *come out of her*!

> The command to "come out of her" in Revelation 18:4 is a warning to God's people to escape the judgment that is to come upon Babylon the Great. The false religious system had her time of influence, when "the kings of the earth committed adultery with her, and the merchants of the earth grew rich from her excessive luxuries" (verse 3). But she is the subject of God's wrath, and she will be judged: "Her sins are piled up to heaven, and YHWH has remembered her crimes" (verse 5). She will suffer a quick demise: "In one day her plagues will overtake her: death, mourning and famine. She will be consumed by fire" (verse 8), and "the great city of Babylon will be thrown down, never to be found again" (verse 21).[17]

If we are going to experience the true abundance of Yahuah (YHWH), we must now realign ourselves to operate out of the Kingdom mindset. A Kingdom mindset means that we align our thoughts, and consequently our lifestyles, with the patterns of the Kingdom and the mind of YHWH. To do this, we must grasp the fact that Our Savior was born a Hebrew, used Hebrew language, and observed Hebrew customs. Therefore, thinking from a Hebraic perspective becomes an important key to unlocking the revelations necessary to shift us into YHWH's ordained system of living. As we seek the Kingdom, it would be wise to ask, "Why did God choose the Hebrew language?" "Why did He make choice of the Hebrew people?" "Why was Abraham chosen to be the Father of the Faith?" I believe the answer lies within God's nature. He is systematic and organized in the way He operates. I believe the Hebrew language is the purposeful medium of creation through which the frequency of Heaven and God Himself can be released into Earth's atmosphere in one of its purest forms. When the frequency of God is released, His desires come to pass in the Earthly dimension. I believe the Israelites, the twelve tribes, and their descendants represent a lineage, which He ordained to propagate the methods by which man was ordained to operate in the Earth realm. They are the literal children of Abraham who came into existence by faith. Faith is the substance of all that comes from God. We must realize that His systems are designed to operate as an extension of Himself and to exclude that which is not of Him.

In scripture, YHWH set forth a foundational mandate to be observed by all believers, which is to celebrate a feast three times a year that is dedicated to Him (Exodus 23:14). These feasts are: the Feast of Unleavened Bread, Pentecost and Tabernacles. The Spring feast season of Unleavened Bread includes three feasts: Passover, Unleavened Bread, and First Fruits. These feasts typify the death, burial and resurrection of Yahushua HaMashiach/Jesus Christ. The Feast of Pentecost signifies the giving of the Holy Spirit. The Fall feast season of Tabernacles includes three feasts: Trumpets, Atonement, and Tabernacles. These feasts typify the return of Christ, Judgment Day, and the Millennial Reign of the Messiah as King). The Bible says:

"And the Lord spake unto Moses, saying, speak unto the children of Israel, and say unto them, Concerning the feasts of YHWH, which ye shall proclaim to be holy convocations, even these are my feasts."

- LEVITICUS 23:1-2

These are not just feasts, but divinely appointed times that YHWH has set to meet with His people. The word, "convocation" means a "gathering" or the "calling of people together". Bringing our mindsets and lifestyles into alignment with YHWH means faithfully honoring the feasts of YHWH. Therefore, to walk in harmony with YHWH through honoring His feasts, we must shift to living by the appointments on the Hebrew calendar that are set by YHWH.

Shabbat – meaning and origin

# Entering into the rest of Elohim is not only a principle of the Kingdom, but a dimension waiting on your arrival.

The Word of YHWH admonishes us to "strive" to enter into His rest through His Shabbat as recorded in Hebrews 4:11.

**Def.: Shabbat**

*noun*

4. The Hebrew word for Sabbath

5. Time of rest.

All YHWH's appointed times are Sabbaths (Shabbats), including weekly, monthly, and annual days that are sanctified as Holy unto the Lord. Weekly Sabbaths, or days of rest, were instituted at creation. The weekly Sabbaths are also moeds (appointed times). Likewise, the feast days are also the moeds. Like the weekly Sabbaths, the feasts are also marked as days of rest.

The balance of this chapter will outline the appointed times/blessing cycles, their Kingdom significance, and how we are called to observe them.

## Days and watches

**DAILY BLESSING CYCLE** - Genesis 1:5 says, *And YHWH called the light Day, and the darkness he called Night. And the evening and the morning were the first day.* On the Gregorian calendar, days begin and end at midnight. On the Gregorian calendar, the days are identified as Monday, Tuesday, Wednesday and so on, all of which are references to pagan gods. On the Hebrew calendar, the day spans from sunset to sunset. Sabbaths and feasts also begin and end from sunset to sunset. The Hebrew calendar identifies each day of the week numerically, "the first day of the week," "the second day of the week," "the third day of the week" and so on as they are referenced in the Bible.

There are hidden Ancient Portals in each day of the Hebrew calendar called "watches." *I will stand upon my watch, and set me upon the tower, and will watch to see what he will say unto me, and what I shall answer when I am reproved* (Habakkuk 2:1).

The Hebrew term "shamar" (to watch, to keep guard, to keep watch) is frequently used throughout scripture, and is used in Genesis 2:15, *Then* YHWH *our Elohim took the man and put him in the garden of Eden to tend and keep it.* The phrase "tend and keep" connotes looking after or taking care of. As we watch over the territory that YHWH has entrusted to us, we are required to follow YHWH's command to rule. YHWH's first command to Adam is to "watch," and that command extends to us today. We are still required to watch.

In the scripture, the term "watch" is also associated with prayer, which is a legal realm where we can adjudicate and legislate based on what YHWH has called us to do. Watching in prayer speaks to a heightened level of spiritual attentiveness to specific issues. When we watch in prayer, we learn to discern spiritual activity and its effect on natural circumstances. It is also during our "watch" that we gather strategies for maintaining dominion and operating in authority.

Understanding the significance of timing is as vital as knowing the importance of decrees. We learn much about timing in Habakkuk 2, where YHWH tells us that we have a watch. Watches are periods of time by which the night and day are divided. Eight prayer-watches are described in the Bible, and we are all allotted a time to pray. During these three-hour periods, we do our best praying and decreeing, as the portal of Heaven is open specifically for us.

You may notice that your prayer-watch changes as seasons transition in your life. Whatever prayer-watch you have, know that each one has a purpose:

**6:00 p.m. to 9:00 p.m.** (1st watch) – This is the first watch of the night. For most people, this is the time after a busy day of work and taking care of the affairs of life. During this time, we tend to relax and reflect over the accomplishments of the day. <u>This is the time to possess the gates of the new day, as each new day begins at sundown on the Biblical Hebrew calendar.</u> It is during this time we are positioned to silence the voice of the wicked one and release the cares of this world as the day comes to a close and a new day begins.

This is a good time to pray for clear direction, for the economy, and for your family. It is also a time of planting the seeds of YHWH's Word through scriptural meditation, causing the Word to take root on the inside of us and become a reality (Lamentations 2:18-19; Matthew 14:15-23; Psalm 59, Psalm 119:148).

**9:00 p.m. to midnight** (2nd watch) – This is the watch prior to the watch when the most spiritual warfare takes place (midnight to 3:00 am). This is the time when intercessors can make significant impact. This is when YHWH deals with the enemies to our destiny.

Pray for favor from men, for the spirit of grace and supplication, for provision to do God's work, and for the release of Angels to go ahead before the spiritual warfare that begins to take place at midnight (Psalm 119:62; Psalm 68:1; Exodus 3:21-11; Exodus 11:3-4, Exodus 12:35-36, Psalm 5:12; Psalm 45:12; Psalm 91:11-12; Hebrews 1:14).

**Midnight to 3:00 a.m.** (3rd watch) – This is the time of heightened spiritual warfare. The powers of darkness take advantage of this time because most people are in deep sleep and are not praying. Matthew 13:25 teaches us that "the enemy sows tares while men sleep." This watch is the time when many problems and casualties can be averted by prayer petitions, which cut off the attack of the enemy before they can do damage.

Pray for protection, provision, and release from demonic strongholds during this time. This watch is also a good time to command release from physical, emotional, psychological, and spiritual prisons, and pray for marriages. Note, this is also a time when dreams, visions, and angelic interventions take place (Mark 1:35; Luke 11:5-13; Judges 16:3; Job 4:13-14; Job 33:15; Acts 16:25-26; Ruth 3:13-14; Matthew 25:6).

**3:00 a.m. to 6:00 a.m.** (4th watch) – This is the last watch of the night; it precedes the first watch of daylight. This is the time when demonic entities are wrapping up their assignments and returning to camp. This also is the time when Yahushua (Jesus) rose to pray according to Mark 1:35. This is the time to speak into the atmosphere what you want to see come to pass.

Pray for the Kingdom of Heaven to come to Earth. Pray that enemies are turned to confusion and decree YHWH's Word. Pray for the release of resurrection power and blessings (Job 22:27-28; Job 38:12-13; Psalm 18:28; Isaiah 60:1-5).

**6:00 a.m. to 9:00 a.m.** (5th prayer watch) – This is the first watch of the day and is the watch when the sun rises. It is a time when YHWH strengthens and heals His people.

Pray for the outpour of Holy Spirit, healing, manifestation of gifts, and for light to overtake darkness (Psalm 103:2-4; Isaiah 60:1-22; Malachi 4:2; Acts 2:15; II Corinthians 9:3; Matthew 5:16).

**9:00 a.m. to noon** (6th watch) – This second watch of the day is when you should expect to see manifestations of what you have prayed for. This is the watch wherein Yahushua (Jesus) was crucified and where you sense that your life is not your own, that you are here for YHWH's purpose and divine use.

Pray for crucifying of the flesh, forgiveness, healing of relationships, harvest, and scientific and technological advances inspired by Holy Spirit (Romans 8:12-15; Colossians 3:2-11; Matthew 6:15; Mark 11:25).

**Noon to 3:00 p.m.** (7th watch) – This midday watch is when most people in the workplace take their period of rest which is often used as a lunch break. It is also the time when the sun is at its highest. It is also one of the three times a day that Daniel prayed. In addition, this is the time of day when Apostle Peter received the vision of the clean and unclean animals which showed the inclusion of the Gentiles into the family of YHWH. It is specifically mentioned in Psalm 91:6 as the time to get into the secret place of the Most High so that you can avoid demonic attacks upon you and your family.

Pray for the Church, new precepts, ideas and ways of doing things; pray that your light shines brighter and brighter. This is a time for dwelling in the secret place of The Most High, to exercise your given dominion as a son or daughter of the Most High, and to enforce YHWH's will, justice and righteousness (Acts 10:9-16; Psalm 91; Matthew 5:16).

**3:00 p.m. to 6:00 p.m.** (8th watch) – This is the fourth watch of the day and is also biblically deemed the "hour of prayer" according to Acts 3:1. 3 o'clock is the ninth hour of the day and the time that Yahushua (Jesus) died on the cross according to Matthew 27:46-51. This is the watch of the day when the trajectory of mankind was changed forever.

Pray for death to self and selfishness. Pray for removal of veils. Pray for removal of limiting belief systems. Pray for the restoration, glory, and blessings of the Father. Pray that you transform and shape history to establish the Kingdom. Pray for the grace to finish strong (Matthew 27:46-51; Luke 23-44-46; 1 John 1:7; Galatians 2:20; Colossians 1:20).

**Daily Meditation** - In Joshua 1:8-9, Joshua is instructed to meditate on the word day and night to create a prosperous way and have good success. The word "meditate" in Hebrew language is "hagad" which means to mull over or make a deep connection with something. It's very interesting that the instruction included "when" to meditate. Why is it important to mull over and make deep connections day and night? Scientific research shows that when our bodies are in lower states of consciousness we are able to access deeper parts of our spiritual being. It's also proven that we reach those lower states of consciousness twice per day. It happens when we first wake up for the day and right before we go to sleep at night. This is why the principle of rest is so critical to creating the life you desire. We should think on, mull over and make a deep connection with what we desire to see in our lives when we first wake up in the morning and right before we drift off to sleep at night.

## Weekly moed - Shabbat

**WEEKLY BLESSING CYCLE** - The Sabbath is the weekly portal whereby we can enter a dimension to be restored, recalibrated, and become more intimately connected with the Father. Shabbat is the original Hebrew word for our English word sabbath. . . and means "to cease, to end, to rest."[18] We should be consistent with our time of Sabbath rest to ensure it is kept holy so that we may grow in our relationship with Him.

According to the scriptures, YHWH rested on the seventh day; so He blessed that day. Genesis 1:1-3 says:

> Thus the heavens and the earth were finished, and all the host of them. And on the seventh day God ended his work which he had made; and he rested on the seventh day from all his work which he had made. And God blessed the seventh day, and sanctified it: because that in it he had rested from all his work which God created and made.

Exodus 20:8-11 says:

> Remember the Sabbath day, to keep it holy. Six days shalt thou labor, and do all thy work: But the seventh day is the Sabbath of YHWH thy Elohim: in it thou shalt not do any work, thou, nor thy son, nor thy daughter, thy manservant, nor thy maidservant, nor thy cattle, nor thy stranger that is within thy gates: For in six days YHWH made heaven and earth, the sea, and all that in them is, and rested the seventh day: wherefore YHWH blessed the Sabbath day, and hallowed it.

YHWH put great emphasis on the weekly Sabbath, as it is referenced in the cycle of creation according Genesis 1:1-3. He then reinforced it with the word, "REMEMBER" the Sabbath day, to keep it holy, in Exodus 20:8. The word "REMEMBER" indicates that YHWH had issued the instruction prior to its recording in this scripture. The only other reference before this scripture is found in Genesis 1:1-3. This infers that the original command to keep the Sabbath is found in the creation cycle. It is clearly stated that the Sabbath is the only day of the week that is "blessed."

We are given six days to labor and do all of our work and we are instructed to rest on the seventh day or the "blessed" day.

YHWH has established the observance of the Sabbath as a sign between He and His people in Exodus 31:16-17 that says:

Wherefore the children of Israel shall keep the Sabbath, to observe the Sabbath throughout their generations, for a perpetual covenant. It is a sign between me and the children of Israel for ever: for in six days YHWH made heaven and earth, and on the seventh day he rested, and was refreshed.

This scripture references the Children of Israel, which speaks of Jacob and his descendants. Abraham was the grandfather to Jacob. Galatians 3:29 makes it clear that those who are of faith are, along with Jacob, among the children of Abraham. It says, *and if ye be Christ's, then are ye Abraham's seed, and heirs according to the promise.* If Sabbath observance is a sign or mark upon the children of Israel, it stands to reason that because we are also children of Abraham, the same applies to us.

Let's look at some Sabbath traditions. Practicing Jews celebrate by lighting a candle on Friday evening. They say a blessing, go to synagogue, come home, say a prayer to sanctify the Shabbat and have dinner. There is a Saturday service, another dinner and personal Torah study. At the end of Shabbat, they say another blessing to begin the next week.[19] I personally do not subscribe to the observance of the Sabbath (Shabbat) in such a ridgid and ritualistic way. I agree with Paul as he made it clear in Colossians 2:16.

# Therefore let no one judge you in regard to food and drink or in regard to (the observance of) a festival or a new moon or a Sabbath day.

This scripture means, don't let anyone judge you on how you observe any Sabbath, whether weekly, monthly, or during holy days. This is not to say that we are not required to follow the ten commandments any longer. Paul is reminding us that we now observe the Sabbath within the context of Yahushua HaMashiach (Jesus Christ). Remember, most Jewish people have not come into the revelation of Yahushua HaMashiach (Jesus Christ). So, for them, this is a law or a way to secure the blessings of YHWH. But, to us the law does not apply. We are not constrained by the law, but rather by the Holy Spirit who lives in us according to Galatians 5:18.

The Bible says to 1) remember the Sabbath, 2) keep it Holy, 3) do no work. Yahushua (Jesus) was known to do good on the Sabbath, thus breaking the law according to the establishment of that day. Yes, He made a habit of going to the synagogue on the seventh day, but He had a different attitude about it. He declared, "I Am the Lord of the Sabbath!" In other words, He is our eternal rest and that is what we should remember as we celebrate the Sabbath. Paul, though he made the point about not judging people regarding observing the Sabbath, was making the same point that Yahushua (Jesus) made. The moedim (appointed times) have nothing to do with rules; they have everything to do with the revelation of Yahushua (Jesus). Though Paul makes a valid point about the change in context concerning Shabbat, he himself did not neglect YHWH's directions concerning remembering the Sabbath and keeping it Holy. Acts 17:2; Acts 13:14, 42, 44; and Acts 16:13 all provide evidence that Paul kept the fourth commandment.

> It was Paul's custom to observe the Sabbath. Paul continued in keeping the Sabbath not just with the Jews but also with the Gentiles. The apostle kept the Sabbath even in gentile cities where there were no synagogues. Paul observed 78 Sabbaths in Corinth persuading both Jews and Greeks (regarding the faith as he taught in the synagogues).[20]

## Benefits of keeping the Sabbath and suggested ways to observe it

> "And he said unto them,
> The Sabbath was made for man,
> and not man for the Sabbath."
>
> MARK 2:27

Much of mankind has been deceived by the world's system into thinking that disobeying this command somehow adds value to us. Out of all the commandments listed in Exodus 20, honoring the Sabbath, and keeping it holy is the one many seem to think is optional. I declare that we shall no longer be deceived!

There are great benefits in observing the Sabbath. From wealth to health, there are blessings that are set in place that operate by the rhythm of seven. The seventh day is blessed because YHWH called it blessed. We must acknowledge the supernatural properties of harmonizing with His weekly blessing cycle. The following are benefits of Sabbath keeping:

1. We are BLESSED when we keep the Sabbath! It may seem like a hard concept to grasp because we are conditioned to think that work creates productivity. However, real productivity comes from a place of REST!

2. The Sabbath allows time for recreation or RE-CREATION! Most people are going through life and allowing life to happen to them without ever taking time to "create" the life that they desire. Creation happens from the place of REST.

   In Genesis 1:26-31, we find where YHWH creates man on the sixth day. So, man's official first full day on Earth as a created being starts on the Sabbath day, the day of rest. On the very next day we see man with the ability to name all of the animals according to Genesis 2:19. So at the point that YHWH's creativity ceased, Adam's creative ability kicked in. After all, he was well rested!

3. The Sabbath reminds us that we are FREE! Historically, the only people who work seven days a week are SLAVES! Deuteronomy 5:15 says, *Remember that you were slaves in Egypt and that YHWH your Elohim brought you out of there with a mighty hand and an outstretched arm. Therefore, YHWH your Elohim has*

*commanded you to observe the Sabbath day.* The simple act of honoring the day of rest ensures that we operate from the realm of sonship not slavery. After all, no good father would have his son working seven days a week. Many are led to believe, by "influencers" on various media platforms that, the good life can only be achieved by working long hard hours. Well, I'm here to tell you today, that even a billionaire who works seven days a week is living like a billionaire slave.

4.  The Sabbath helps with developing and growing relationships! Because there is no work on the Sabbath, observers can share more time with family and friends. It is a time when we can shut off our mind from things associated with our jobs and careers and give undivided attention to those who are most important to us — our family, friends and loved ones. It is customary in the Jewish community to spend the Sabbath celebrating with family and friends. Jewish people and Mormons have the highest rates of marriage and the lowest rates of divorce. This has been partly attributed to the quality time they share with their families on the Sabbath.

5.  The Sabbath is a day of rest. Most people who keep the Sabbath will not only defer from doing any work that brings personal gain, but they will not wash the car, wash dishes, clean the house, wash clothes, etc. They do no work and this is a good thing. Rest extends life expectancy! This is because it provides time for every cell, organ, muscle, tissue, chemical and system in the body to be

restored. Our bodies are intimately connected to our minds and an overworked body leads to an overworked mind, which leads to stress.

According to the American Psychological Association, chronic stress is linked to the six leading causes of death: heart disease, cancer, lung ailments, accidents, cirrhosis of the liver and suicide. And more than 75 percent of all physician office visits are for stress-related ailments and complaints.[21]

As we consider these benefits, let's make the connection to Ancient Portals. Keeping Shabbat (the Sabbath) opens portals of 1) supernatural prosperity, 2) re-creation through the resurrection power of Christ, 3) the Spirit of Freedom and Liberation by Holy Spirit, 4) the love of Christ in our relationships, and 5) supernatural peace/shalom.

Thank you Father, for Your goodness is great toward us. It is so exciting to realize how Our Heavenly Father purposely used the weekly blessing cycle to open ancient portals for His children. One of my favorite Sabbath scriptures, Isaiah 58:13-14 says,

If thou turn away thy foot from the Sabbath, from doing thy pleasure on my holy day; and call the Sabbath a delight, the holy of YHWH, honorable; and shalt honor him, not doing thine own ways, nor finding thine own pleasure, nor speaking thine own words: Then shalt thou delight thyself in YHWH; and I will cause thee to ride upon the high places of the earth, and feed thee with the heritage of Jacob thy father: for the mouth of YHWH hath spoken it.

This verse gives the key to opening ancient portals on a cycle every seven days. The Sabbath was instituted by YHWH at creation, and it has been Holy ever since. He never changed it. Yahushua never changed it. The Apostles did not change it. And Paul, who emphasized freedom in Christ, did not change it. The Catholic church, beginning with Constantine, who published the Edict of Milan, established freedom of religion and Sunday as the Sabbath. Later, the Council Laodicea declared Saturday (the seventh day) a day of work. Evidence indicates that the switch may have been due to a desire to merge pagan customs with the customs of the Christian faith and establish the papacy as the supreme authority above all others.

The weekly Sabbath should be a joyful time. We should be smiling, enjoying nature, getting extra rest, eating good food, enjoying family and friends and keeping the goodness of YHWH in the forefront of our minds. Also, this is a great time to witness; inviting people over to share a Sabbath meal can be a wonderful opportunity to help ensure that your family, friends, and acquaintances also have a personal relationship with Our Lord and Savior.

The following are some ways that you may choose to observe the Sabbath (as Holy Spirit leads):

- Greet others with the blessing – "Shabbat Shalom" meaning Peaceful Sabbath, or Shavua Tov (have a good week).
- Delight yourself in YHWH with prayer, Bible study, worship, meditation, music, singing, etc.
- Take the day to rest.

- Have a family dinner.

- Recite Isaiah 58:13-14.

- Give to the poor.

- Give an offering to YHWH; the seventh day is blessed, therefore the act of giving offerings would be in alignment with the seven-day cycle of blessing).

- Say a prayer to welcome in the Sabbath on Friday evening, Jewish people also light candles on Friday before Sabbat dinner with their families.

- Take communion as an act of remembrance.

- Give thanks for everything He has done this week and bless the week to come.

- Ask Holy Spirit to visit you and give you revelation on what you should do the next week or concerning YHWH's will for your life.

- Attend an in-person or virtual group Bible study or worship service.

- Play worship music or blow the shofar.

- Take a walk, go to the park, or enjoy nature.

- According to the Yahushua's example, despite obvious objections of non-Messianic Jews (those who do not believe in Yahushua (Jesus), good works would also be permissible on the Shabbat.

Before we move on the to the next Blessing Cycle, I want to deal with the "big elephant in the room". The question of "when" should we observe the Sabbath?

In scripture, the Sabbath is observed on the seventh day of the week, which is Saturday and the scripture cannot be broken. (John 10:35) As a ministry, we honored the Sabbath according to religious traditions, worshipping as a congregation, for seventeen years on Sundays. Although we were faithful to honor and keep the other Holy Days, we neglected the original holy day that starts the cycle of blessings connected to the ancient portals. It was the advent of the pandemic (COVID), when I knew the way, we did ministry would never be the same. In seeking YHWH for what moving forward would look like, He opened the eyes of our understanding to look at our Sabbath worship in a new way. In all honesty, I have celebrated the Sabbath on Friday evenings, at home with family, for years but never made the connection that we should honor it as a ministry as well. This goes to show you the power of the traditions of men making YHWH's word ineffective. I certainly thank YHWY for His grace and bringing our ministry into this new revelation. YHWH went even further to confirm that moving to Saturday worship was the right decision by sending a witness to our congregation from Israel. See the Youtube video by Dr. Kenny Russell of Bulldozer Faith Ministries on October 15, 2022. (https://www.youtube.com/watch?v=KONWW8qyKGA).

## Monthly moed – Rosh Choldesh

**MONTHLY BLESSING CYCLE** – There is a hidden ancient portal in the observance of Rosh Chodesh. Rosh Chodesh literally means "beginning, head, renewal, or restoration" and is the beginning or head of the month. It is a celebration of YHWH's gift of redemption. [22] The Hebrew calendar is based on lunar cycles. Rosh Chodesh, sometimes spelled Kadesh, is a moed (appointed time) that occurs every new moon, which marks the first day of each new month. Rosh Chodesh is a time of new beginnings. It is so powerful to think that with every new month you have the opportunity for a do over! You have the power through the spirit to open portals that will eradicate undesirable outcomes of the past month and project blessings into the new month. It is like a supernatural reset. AND – with that, each new month brings with it new opportunities specific to that month. For example, the month of Adar, which occurs toward the end of February or the beginning of March, is considered the happiest time of the year. Called the month of double joy, it is a time when the Jewish people celebrate the victory of Esther over the evil Haman. The word Adar means strength. This reminds us that the joy of YHWH is our strength. The letter associated with the month is "kuf," the symbol of laughter. It is also associated with the tribe of Naphtili, which means to win the fight or win by resting. There are lots of other symbols associated with that month as well. There is so much symbolism associated with each month that it presents a wonderful opportunity to delve deeper into the things of YHWH and His Word. With every detail the Holy Spirit reveals comes new revelations that are keys to opening Ancient Portals. There are four key points that I would like to make to help you understand the significance of Rosh Chodesh.

**ONE** - Scriptures teach us that the first day of each month was a time to expect divine revelation and strategies from the Lord.

Examples:

> "Another message came to me from the Lord on the first day of the
> month, in the eleventh year (after King Jehoiachin was taken away
> to captivity)."
> EZEKIEL 26:1 (TLB)

> "In the twenty-seventh year, in the first month, on the first day
> of the month, God's Message came to me: "Son of man, Nebu-
> chadnezzar, king of Babylon, has worn out his army against Tyre.
> They've worked their fingers to the bone and have nothing to show
> for it."
> EZEKIEL 29:17-18 (MSG)

> "On the first day of the sixth month of the second year in the
> reign of King Darius of Persia, God's Message was delivered by the
> prophet Haggai to the governor of Judah, Zerubbabel son of Sheal-
> tiel, and to the high priest, Joshua son of Jehozadak."
> HAGGAI 1:1 (MSG)

**TWO** - Rosh Chodesh was a day that was set apart for sacrifice, worship, fellowship and giving unto YHWH. Now that WE are the temple, Rosh Chodesh is even more powerful and important. The following scriptures give insight . . .

> "I am about to build a temple for YHWH my Elohim," Solomon
> told Hiram. "It will be a place where I can burn incense and sweet
> spices before YHWH, and display the special sacrificial bread,
> and sacrifice burnt offerings each morning and evening, and on
> the Sabbaths, and at the new moon celebration and other regular
> festivals of YHWH our Elohim. For Elohim wants Israel always to

celebrate these special occasions.

-II CHRONICLES 2:4 (TLB)

"For as the new heavens and the new earth, which I will make, shall remain before me, saith YHWH, so shall your seed and your name remain. And it shall come to pass, that from one new moon to another, and from one sabbath to another, shall all flesh come to worship before me, saith YHWH."

- ISAIAH 66:22-23

**THREE** - Each month has a supporting tribe, stone, star, alphabet, physical sense, and bodily organ associated with it. See the chart in the additional sources section in the back of this book.

**FOUR** - Rosh Chodesh is celebrated by both men and women, but has a special connection to women. It is said that when the children of Israel were building the golden calf in the wilderness, the women refused to give their jewelry to build the idol. For this reason, women often have the spotlight placed on them during Rosh Chodesh. Women are encouraged to rest from doing some daily tasks and enjoying special recognition by their husbands, family, and community, and participating in women's groups that get together to study and fellowship.

## Annual moeds – YHWH's Feast Days

**ANNUAL BLESSING CYCLES** – Like days that start at nightfall and end at nightfall, and months that start on the new moon, annual holidays on the Hebrew calendar are different from the cycle of holidays on the Gregorian calendar. On the Gregorian calendar, the days start at 12:00 am (midnight) and the first of the month falls on a day that do not align with the new moon. Likewise, annual holidays on the Gregorian calendar represent replacements for YHWH's commanded annual moedim (appointed times). For example, Easter is a merger of the spring festival associated with the goddess of Spring, Eastra and the moed (appointed time) of Passover. Together, they have come together to create a new celebration called Easter (named for Eastra) that includes Easter bunnies, Easter egg hunts, a sunrise worship service at church, etc. Needless to say, it is not a good idea for man to take it upon himself to supersede the commandments of YHWH's. There are many judgments associated with doing so, but one of them is forfeiting the blessing cycle. As you continue reading you will see that there are blessings associated with each of YHWH's feasts, which are to be held annually. Also note that each new year on the Hebraic calendar is represented by a number which reveals a prophecy for that year.

Every year, YHWH wants to accomplish specific things in our lives to move us forward into destiny. When we know what YHWH is saying about the season we are in, we can prosper in any season! YHWH's plan is always to bring us into the blessing.

## Example of prophetic number for the New Year

The year 2023 on the Hebrew calendar is 5783. These are cycles of years. Currently, the Biblical calendar 2023/5783 denotes that we are in the second year of a ten-year cycle which began in 2020/5780. The Hebrew calendar year 5783 denotes that there have been 5,783 years since the creation of the Earth. The Hebrew letter for "8" is "PEY." The letter "PEY" is shaped like a mouth, which tells us that this ten-year cycle has something to do with the mouth prophetically. The entire decade is about the "MOUTH", "SPEECH, "SPEAKING. The number "3" is depicted by the letter "GIMEL" which looks like a camel. The number 3 indicates that the third year in the decade of "PEY" or third year in the decade of the "MOUTH" is the year of never-ending supply. This also corresponds to Isaiah 60:6, which says that Herds of camels will cover your land, young camels of Midian and Ephah. And all from Sheba will come, bearing gold and incense and proclaiming the praise of the LORD.

It would take a book to unpack the symbolism that is revealed in each of the numbers for each year. It is so deep, but also so simple. It's like YHWH really desires for His children to know His secrets. The truth of the matter is HE DOES!!! This is one of the benefits of obediently entering into His timetable by observing the calendar that He ordained.

## Keeping the feasts is a commandment

Also, hidden in the Hebrew calendar is a cycle of festivals that are divine appointments established by YHWH. These appointments are not optional but required by all believers. Even though the feast days are often called the "Jewish festivals", YHWH clearly intended for these divine appointments to be observed by all His children, including the non-Jews who would believe upon Him through Yahushua HaMashiach, Jesus. The scripture says:

And the Lord spake unto Moses, saying, Speak unto the children of
Israel, and say unto them, Concerning the feasts of the Lord, which
ye shall proclaim to be holy convocations, even these are My feasts.
LEVITICUS 23:1-2 (NIV)

These are the Lord's appointed festivals, the sacred assemblies you
are to proclaim at their appointed times.
LEVITICUS 23:4

And ye shall observe the feast of unleavened bread; for in this
selfsame day have I brought your armies out of the land of Egypt:
therefore shall ye observe this day in your generations by an ordi-
nance forever.
EXODUS 12:17

And ye shall keep it a feast unto the LORD seven days in the year.
It shall be a statute forever in your generations.
LEVITICUS 23:41

## Jesus observed the Feasts

When Yahushua (Jesus) had finished saying all these things, he said
to his disciples, 2 "As you know, the Passover is two days away—and the Son
of Man will be handed over to be crucified. Matthew 26:1-2

On the first day of the Festival of Unleavened Bread, the disciples
came to Yahushua (Jesus) and asked, "Where do you want us to make prepa-
rations for you to eat the Passover? Matthew 26:17

## Seven feasts

The Hebrew calendar honors holy days that were instituted by the Yahuah - Passover, Unleavened Bread, First Fruits, Pentecost, Trumpets (Rosh Hashanah), Day of Atonement (Yom Kippur), and Tabernacles (Leviticus 23). In contrast, the Gregorian Calendar recognizes holidays which the Roman emperor Constantine used to subvert these holy days. We see here the same tactic of the enemy – take truth, pervert it, and present it in a manipulative way. So overall, to stay syncopated with the rhythmic flow of Heaven's timetable, it is necessary for believers to remember to honor YHWH's holy days and not lay aside His commandments for the traditions of men (Mark 7:8-9).

There are seven major annual feast days on the Jewish calendar, as stated earlier. There are three feasts together in the Spring feast season, Passover, Unleavened Bread, and First Fruits, which typify the death, Burial and resurrection of our Lord and Savior Yahushua HaMashiach (Jesus Christ). There is one feast to itself, Pentecost. Pentecost (the feast of Weeks) takes place 50 days after Passover and coincides with the wheat harvest and is the celebration of the giving of the gift of the Holy Spirit, Ruach Hakodesh. There are three feasts together in the fall, Trumpets, Atonement, and Tabernacles, which typify the return of Christ, the necessity to be ready for the Day of Judgment, and the Millennial Reign.

# Understanding the New Year(s)

To add perspective to the annual cycles of YHWH it is good to understand that the Jewish people observe four (4) New Years. This implies that they observe four calendars. They are as follows:

**ROSH HASHANAH (MARKS THE BIRTH OF CREATION AND IS THE CIVIL NEW YEAR)** - Rosh Hashanah in Hebrew means "head of the year." Rosh Hashanah occurs during the month of Tishrei around the end of September or the first part of October. It is the celebration of the birthday of the Universe and the creation of Adam and Eve. This is the beginning of the yearly cycle for the keeping of years and accounting purposes. "The First of Tishrei is the New Year for years, of the years of release and Jubilee years and for planting and vegetables.[23]" The years of release, Jubilee years, and even Shmita years are cycles of time such as every 7 years or every 50 years, when YHWH mandated that debts be forgiven, or the fields were not to be worked. These 50- and 7-year cycles are worth studying. I have not included the study of these cycles to purposefully keep the revelations in this book as comprehensible as possible. As engrafted believers, we should observe the Hebraic civil calendar.

**THE FIRST OF NISAN (MARKS THE RELIGIOUS/ BIBLICAL/ SACRED NEW YEAR)** - Nisan is referenced as the "head of months" and is the first of the months according to the Bible. This is the beginning of the yearly cycle for the keeping of YHWH's appointed times. It comes about around the end of March and the first part of April. Nisan is the month of the celebration of Passover. Yahuah set this month as the beginning of the year in Exodus 12:2 that says, "This month shall be for you the head of months, the first of the months of the year" (Exodus 12:2). "The 1st of Nisan is the new year for kings and festivals.[24]" As engrafted believers, we should observe the Hebraic Religious/Biblical calendar as commanded in the scriptures.

**TU B'SHEVAT (MARKS THE BIRTH OF TREES)** - Tu B'Shevat marks the birthday of trees and is a time to focus on planting and nurturing these life-giving organisms. The name means 15th of Shevat, which is the month this holiday occurs.

Today, Tu B'Shevat is celebrated as an ecological holiday or a "Jewish Earth Day", where some celebrate by learning about trees and climate justice. This is not a calendar that we as believers observe generally.

ELUL (MARKS THE HEAD OF THE MONTH AND THE NEW YEAR OF ANIMALS) - Elul is the last month of the year and is a time of sanctification in preparation for the next month Tishrei, the month filled with high holidays. "The 1st of Elul is the new year for the cattle tithe [25]" This is not a calendar that we as believers observe generally.

NOTE – To better understand, the concept of the Jewish people having multiple calendars, we may consider that a similar system of multiple calendars is also used on the Gregorian calendar. For example, on the Gregorian calendar, the civil calendar is observed by the general population and the fiscal calendar is observed by businesses and organizations for financial accounting purposes.

YHWH's times and seasons are supernatural. The Sons of Issachar understood the times and the seasons, and they knew what to tell the Israelites to do. They were wealthy. They were one of the lead tribes and helped the Israelites win key battles. By studying the times and seasons of YHWH and His appointed times and even the signs in the Heavens, we will be able to operate in continuous cycles of YHWH's blessings and navigate the end times in which we live.

# CHAPTER EIGHT

# ASTRONOMY NOT ASTROLOGY: TIMES & SEASONS

> *Astronomy is the naturally occurring science that studies the heavens. This is not the same as astrology.*

THE STUDY OF THE HEAVENS – Today, many are mixing occult and demonic practices with Christian faith, specifically astrology which often gets confused with astronomy. Hence, it is imperative as a follower of Yahushua HaMashiach (Jesus Christ) that you understand the difference between astronomy and astrology. So, let's first discuss astronomy.

To mature in faith and comprehend the impacts of astronomy, you must first know who you are in YHWH and understand the heavens. The Bible declares that those who allow themselves to be led by the spirit of YHWH are the sons of YHWH, heirs with Christ, and share in His spiritual inheritance (Romans 8:14-17). The Bible also affirms that because we are in Christ, we are seated with Him in heavenly places (Ephesians 2:6). Consequently, it is our divine right and inheritance to understand, interpret, and access the heavens. Now, the Hebrew word for heavens as described in Genesis 1 is "*hashamyim*", meaning the nested heavens. Understanding this concept makes us cognizant that there is not just the heaven where YHWH the Father and Yahushua (Jesus) are, but that there are multiple heavens (this is why YHWH called the firmament or the expanse of sky "Heaven" in Genesis 1:8). Therefore, you should embrace the study of the heavens, which is astronomy.

Specifically, astronomy is the naturally occurring science that studies the heavens and deals with heavenly bodies (the sun, moon, stars, planets, galaxies, etc.), their motions, magnitude, distances, and physical constitution. Considering this and taking into account that the heavens are the handiwork of YHWH, and they belong to him (Psalm 8:3, 102:25, 115:16), we must acknowledge that the sun, moon, stars, constellations, and other heavenly bodies were not given for a sinister purpose or for the study of witchcraft. YHWH gave them to us so that we may gain deeper insight into his timing, seasons, movement, patterns, magnitude, scope, speed, expanse, structure, and ways. To bring further clarity, let's look at passages of scripture where we see astronomy and astronomical influences, which were used for revelation, confirmation, impartation, transportation, and navigation.

# STARS AND CONSTELLATIONS

He who made the Pleiades and Orion and turns deep darkness into the morning and darkens the day into night, who calls for the waters of the sea and pours them out on the surface of the earth, the Lord is His name.
- AMOS 5:8 (ESV)

Amos, who was a herdsman and prophet, reveals God's mind, sovereignty, and creative power (just as stated in Joel 2:30 and Amos 4:13), through the signs and wonders of heavenly bodies that are made by YHWH. Through the observing and study of the stars, Amos tells the names of constellations (an area where clusters of stars form a recognizable pattern) in the heavens such as Orion and the Pleiades (a group of 7 stars found within the constellation Taurus), which is additionally referenced in Job 9:8-9. His observation also brings confirmation to Psalm 147:4 and Isaiah 40:26 that says YHWH "calls the stars by their names."

# IMAGES IN THE CONSTELLATIONS -

Canst thou bind the sweet influences of Pleiades, or loose the bands of Orion? Canst thou bring forth Mazzaroth in his season?
- JOB 38:31-32

The word "Mazzaroth" used in this passage of scripture is a Hebrew word for zodiac and means constellation or signs. Constellations are groups of stars that form pictures. These pictures detail the story of YHWH's plan of salvation and His return as described throughout the scriptures. There is also a path or way called the ecliptic (Zodiac) that the sun follows through the sky in a year. This is where the 12 major constellations originate from. They begin with the Virgin, which goes back to Genesis 3:15 where YHWH tells the serpent he will put enmity between him and the woman, and ends with the Lion, which goes back to the Lion of Judah, the Messiah, in Revelation 5:5, Genesis 49:8-9, and Numbers 24:8-9. Bearing these things in mind, it is crucial as a Believer to understand that constellations are not astrological signs, but signs that are given by YHWH concerning Him and His people.

## KNOWLEDGE FROM THE HEAVENS –

The heavens declare the glory of YHWH; And the firmament sheweth his handiwork. Day unto day uttereth speech, and night unto night sheweth knowledge. There is  no speech nor language, where their voice is not heard. Their line is gone out through all the earth, And their words to the end of the world.  In them hath he set a tabernacle for the sun, Which is as a bridegroom coming out of his chamber, and rejoiceth as a strong man to run a race. His going forth is from the end of the heaven, and his circuit unto the ends of it:

- PSALM 19:1-6

This passage of scripture is referring to the heavens, stars, and knowledge. Groups of stars have names and images that go along with them, which are reflected in the heavens. In ancient times many people were only acquainted with stars and the images that went along with them. This is why the voice of the stars are heard in all speech and all languages because like love and pain, pictures speak their own universal language, and these pictures can be seen from anywhere in the world. The scriptures above also communicate that revelatory knowledge can be gained from the heavens and heavenly bodies. Certain happenings that occur in these constellation sign images are telling the story of the return of Yahushua HaMashiach (Jesus Christ) and speak to various prophetic events.

# THE MAGI –

After Jesus was born in Bethlehem in Judea, during the time of king Herod, Magi from the east came to Jerusalem and asked, "Where is the one who has been born king of the Jews? We saw his star when it rose and have come to worship him." When king Herod heard this he was disturbed, and all Jerusalem with him. When he had called together all the people's chief priests and teachers of the law, he asked them where the Messiah was to be born. "In Bethlehem in Judea" they replied, "for this is what the prophet has written: "'But you the rulers of Judah; for out of you will come a ruler who will shepherd my people Israel.'" Then Herod called the Magi secretly and found out from them the exact time the star had appeared. He sent them to Bethlehem and said "Go and search carefully for the child. As soon as you find him, report to me, so that I too may go and worship him". After they had heard the king, they went on their way, and the star they had seen when it rose went ahead of them until it stopped over the place where the child was. When they saw the star, they were overjoyed.

- MATTHEW 2:1-10 (NIV)

The Magi were scholars and mathematicians that were skilled in astronomy to the point where they were able to tell the times and seasons like the sons of Issachar (I Chronicles 12:32) and get revelation by looking into the constellations. It is thought that the Magi were the descendants of the sons of Issachar. Through the portal in the star of the heavens, they were transported into another dimension whereby revelatory knowledge was imparted to accurately navigate them to the birthplace of Yahushua HaMashiach (Jesus Christ) and confirm the words written by the prophet.

Ultimately, pure astronomy reveals YHWH and brings us into harmony with Him. It is important for believers to know that the studying of the heavens can bring revelation knowledge that should always lead you to align yourself with YHWH and worship Him. In a like manner, it is just as essential to recognize that satan always desires to pervert what YHWH gives. The Bible clearly depicts that satan is the father of lies, a teller of half-truths, and a skilled manipulator. In the garden, satan came up to Eve and started a conversation with the intention of manipulating her into believing that if she ate of a specific tree she would be like YHWH, when she was already made in the image and likeness of YHWH (Genesis 1:26-27, 3:1-5). Satan also tried to manipulate Yahushua (Jesus) in the wilderness by telling Him that he would give Him all the inhabited kingdoms of the earth if He worshiped him (Luke 4:5-7), despite the fact that it is already pre-destined that "the kingdoms of this world are become the kingdoms of our Lord and of his Christ" (Revelation 11:15). These two examples demonstrate a key tactic in satan's overarching agenda to steal, kill, and destroy. This tactic is to take truth, pervert it, and present it in a manipulative way so that people are subjugated to be imprisoned by the kingdom of darkness. Today the same tactic is used with Astronomy. The enemy takes the truth of what YHWH gave (Astronomy), perverts it, and manipulatively presents it as astrology.

## *The perversion of astronomy is astrology*

Astrology is not a naturally occurring science but a type of divination (the art of mystic insight or fortune telling) by the stars because it seeks knowledge of the future or the unknown by supernatural means. You see, the supernatural or spiritual realm is not just one-sided. You have two kingdoms, the Kingdom of YHWH and the kingdom of darkness. Therefore, just as there are portals to access that which is holy, there are portals to access that which is satanic or evil. Astrology is a satanic portal into the kingdom of darkness for several reasons.

Astrology perverts the constellations given by YHWH because false deities were made from the images of the constellations. So, astrology becomes a practice that originates out of false worship, thereby making anyone who studies astrology an idolater because they exchange the glory and truth of YHWH for an idol and a lie (Romans 1:21-25). Astrology also shifts the focus from the Lord to human beings because it makes people look for who they are and seek out their destinies outside of the purposes of YHWH. It opens the door for people to become sucked into a satanic world through astrological sweet talk or flattering divination, which leads directly away from the truth of YHWH's word that states we are made in His likeness and are the Lord's instruments set apart for His use (Genesis 1:26-27; I Peter 2:9). In addition to this, astrology also involves other satanic, new age, and occult practices such as tarot cards, witch instruction manuals, magic, fortunetelling, psychics, clairvoyance, spiritualism, and mysticism. All of these practices are mediums that bring information through contact with the evil side of the spirit realm and anoints people to carry out the evil desires of their father, the devil.

Now when looking to scripture, YHWH commands believers to never listen to or be involved with any type of divination (Deuteronomy 18:9-14; II Kings 17:12-17; Jeremiah 27:9, 29:8). In Acts 16, Paul cast the spirit of divination, a python spirit, out of a slave girl (Acts 16:16). The "spirit of the python" is a territorial, lying, manipulative, choking spirit. So, this reveals in totality why believers should never be or get involved with divination practices. Not only is it an abomination to YHWH, but it is an evil spirit that comes to choke the "Spirit of Truth" out of you and manipulate you into losing your place with YHWH!

# CHAPTER NINE

# NONE EMPTY HANDED

> *There are protocols, principles, methods, technologies, and procedures that govern everything in His Kingdom and His system of giving is no different.*

W hen we think about seedtime and harvest, we think of cycles. As a rule, you will always reap more than you sow. Even as it pertains to creation, everything starts with a seed. Whether it is a thought, idea, word, or deed, a literal seed or giving of one's resources, seeds are YHWH's method of sustaining life and expanding the Earthly dimension. Seeds are keys to other dimensions that open doors and gates. Even humans cannot enter the Earthly dimension without the seed of the father. Thus, this book would not be complete without addressing how seeds are used to access ancient portals.

*Ancient portal*

> *"Wisdom is the principal thing; therefore get wisdom: and with all thy getting get understanding."* – PROVERBS 4:7

Sadly, in the body of Christ there are many instances when believers feel abandoned by YHWH because they don't see His blessings in their lives. Consequently, they are left with the questions of "Where are my blessings" or "Where is my harvest"? If you have found yourself or find yourself asking these very same questions, you must realize that YHWH is not a bad parent. He didn't leave you out of His will. In John 10:10, Yahushua/Jesus says, "A thief is only there to steal, kill, and destroy. I came so that they can have real and eternal life, more and better life than they ever dreamed of." YHWH loves us with an everlasting love and never desires to see us lack or beg for anything. What is lacking is the full knowledge and thorough understanding of YHWH's system of giving, which is necessary to ensure our prosperity and enjoyment of the abundant life He promised us right here on earth. So, please listen carefully as I make this statement:

# Everything about YHWH is strategic; nothing is done haphazardly.

There are protocols, principles, methods, technologies, and procedures that govern everything in His Kingdom and His system of giving is no different. To grow in wisdom and experience YHWH's cycle of blessings in your everyday life, you must first have a firm understanding of this system's framework.

A system is generally defined as a set of things working together as parts of a mechanism or a set of principles or procedures according to which something is done. YHWH's system of giving consists of specified ancient portals that work in tandem with the network of Heaven that will allow you to experience a constant inflow of the Father's manifested blessings on a continual basis. As depicted below, there are three subsets of ancient portals that comprise YHWH's System of Giving: Offering, Tithe, and Firstfruit.

In this system there are at least three people involved: the giver, the receiver, and YHWH. The giver and the receiver are both important factors in the system. However, Acts 20:35 details that it is "more blessed to give than to receive." Therefore, in this context, let's focus on the giver as we discuss these three ancient portals.

## Offerings

We see offerings present all throughout scripture. Offerings are gifts that people present before YHWH in worship or devotion to Him that are separate from the tithe. Our offerings should display that Jesus is Lord of our lives, be an expression from our being of gratitude to the Father and be a by-product of our worship that brings a sweet-smelling savor before God. Ultimately, offerings (like seeds) are an ancient portal that opens the door for the cycle of blessings to operate in our lives. Let's first look at Proverbs 11:24-25 (AMP):

> There is the one who (generously) scatters (abroad), and yet
> increases all the more; And there is the one who withholds what
> is justly due, but it results only in want and poverty. The generous

man (is a source of blessing and) shall be prosperous and enriched, and he who waters will himself be watered (reaping the generosity he has sown).

In this passage of scripture, the Bible signifies the principle of reaping, sowing, and that we are in return blessed with the measure we use to give to others. In a like manner, it also reveals that an offering of generosity is the portal that opens the door for us to become the housing mechanism and source for: prosperity, increase, and the blessings of God. The reason we become the embodiment of this scripture in the earth is because the Holy Spirit of YHWH lives in us (I Corinthians 3:16). Therefore, the One who provides provision, living water and the economy of heaven is in you. However, when you withhold what is justly due to YHWH, the spirit of what you withheld becomes your god and in turn gains residency rights. Consequently, the life nourishing spring of water (The Holy Spirit) and the economy of YHWH that were in you (sustaining you) evaporates, eliminating the power for you to: water, be watered, and move in abundance. Your ability to water and be watered is your ability to bless others and be blessed. Yet, when you do not operate properly in YHWH's system of giving, as a result, you begin to operate with an impoverished spirit and mind, essentially causing self-bankruptcy, leading to deficits due to your own poor decision. Beyond this passage of scripture, we can see multiple revelatory insights regarding offerings in II Corinthians 9:6-11 (AMPC):

[6] (Remember) this: he who sows sparingly and grudgingly will also reap sparingly and grudgingly, and he who sows generously (that blessings may come to someone) will also reap generously and with blessings. [7] Let each one (give) as he has made up his own mind and purposed in his heart, not reluctantly or sorrowfully or under compulsion, for YHWH loves (He takes pleasure in, prizes above other things, and is unwilling to abandon or to do without) a cheerful (joyous, "prompt to do it") giver (whose heart is in his giving). [8] And YHWH is able to make all grace (every favor and earthly blessing) come to you in abundance, so that you may always and under all circumstances and whatever the need be self-sufficient (possessing enough to require no aid or support and furnished in abundance for every good work and charitable donation). [9] As it is written, He (the benevolent person) scatters abroad; He gives to the poor; His deeds of justice and goodness and kindness and benevolence will go on and endure forever! [10] And (YHWH) Who provides seed for the sower and bread for eating will also provide and multiply your (resources for) sowing and increase the fruits of your righteousness (which manifests itself in active goodness, kindness, and charity). [11] Thus you will be enriched in all things and in every way, so that you can be generous, and (your generosity as it is) administered by us will bring forth thanksgiving to YHWH.

Looking closely here, the words "sparingly" and "grudgingly" in the above scripture reveals a key tactic of the enemy to kill God's influence, steal your ability to receive bountiful blessings, and destroy your power to be a kingdom financier in the earth. The word sparingly means "in a restricted manner" and the word grudgingly means "reluctant", which is an open door to doubt. The only way doubt can get implanted in the mind of the Believer is if the devil makes an offering. Yes! The devil makes offerings too! The devil offers you doubt and when you accept his offering, doubt immediately restricts the vats of heaven that releases the overflow of YHWH from being poured out upon you and multiplying your resources. So not only are you restricting heaven, but you are now restricted from receiving every favor and earthly blessing because your receiving is predicated on your giving. In addition to this, the people you are supposed to minister to through giving generous offerings are no longer able to be blessed by you. Do you see how the enemy works? Essentially, the devil seeks to destroy your ability to be a kingdom distributor and alter the genome of YHWH within you because the principle of giving willingly is woven into the fabric of who YHWH is.

The words "sparingly" and "grudgingly" (along with other words) also unveil two revelatory keys hidden in scripture. These words speak to both giving and the posture of the giver's heart. Giving and the posture (the attitude, stance, position, and strength) of the heart of the giver work in tandem together to present an offering before God. The attitude of your heart matters when giving because your attitude is a part of your essence, the make-up of who you are on the inside. When your insides protrude to your outer man, you emit a specific smell. Just like you emit a smell in the natural world, you also emit a smell spiritually. Spiritually, when you give with a begrudging attitude you emit a repulsively foul smell. But, when the attitude of your heart aligns with the posture of the Lord's heart, YHWH no longer smells you because now all He can smell is Himself. So, when He smells that sweet smelling savor, your offering then becomes acceptable, and he opens the windows of heaven to pour you out blessings that you do not have room enough to receive.

Never forget, giving just puts the key in the lock, but aligning your heart-posture with YHWH's heart-posture turns the key to open the door to the cycle of God's blessings. Now even though this portal's activating keys are clearly shown in scripture, the truth is that many want to reap the blessings of God, but they don't want to take part in God's process that leads to His harvest (which is typical of a religious spirit). You see, the heart of YHWH is to take on the process that leads to the promise. Let's take Jesus as our example. The resurrection, ascension, seating of Jesus, and giving of the promised Holy Spirit could not happen until his death happened. He had to not just give his life but give it willingly.

Yahushua/Jesus said in Luke 22:42, *Father, if thou be willing, remove this cup from me: nevertheless, not my will, but thine, be done.* That "nevertheless" was the posture of Jesus' heart being transmitted through his will, which was the root of his willingness. The willingness of Jesus to take on the heart of the Father led him to operate in a blessed dimension called "joy" and be imparted with supernatural strength by the angel to endure the cross for the goal of conquering satan and reconciling us back to YHWH again. This is the whole point of the commandment to give cheerfully, joyfully, and willingly. It is Jesus' heart being transmitted through your will, causing you to take on the process that leads to His promises. Religion has taught us to leave everything up to God, but the life of Jesus teaches us the same principle that is exemplified in II Corinthians 9, that some things are just simply a decision. YHWH is not going to coerce, pressure, or force you to give. You must make up your own mind. Do you want to experience God's cycle of blessings, or do you want to give in accordance with the voice of your flesh? The choice is yours, but I beseech you to operate in God's system of giving because it yields extraordinary returns. Ecclesiastes 11:1 (MSG) says: "Be generous: Invest in acts of charity, charity yields high returns."

You become invested in acts of charity when you give of your resources (financial and non-financial). Matching this with an attitude of generosity allows you to take on the posture of the heart of the Lord. So, in essence, your offering is the portal that manifests the glory of YHWH in every area of your life above what you can even ask or imagine. This is where you experience the supernatural blessings of The Almighty that allow you to taste and see that the Lord is good! On the other hand, when you do not follow this pattern outlined in scripture, you become the embodiment of Luke 8:14. You hear the word of YHWH but not with the spirit of understanding (which is why the Bible says take heed to how you hear), and your immaturity causes you to be choked by the riches of this life leading to loss. Why? Because you've become a hoarder and your hoarded treasures become treasures of darkness, which YHWH promises to give to His people (along with the hidden riches of secret places) in accordance with Isaiah 45:3.

## Tithes

Many have become apostates and fallen into heretical strange doctrines that teach against tithing, especially because we are under grace through Jesus Christ. What is taught is "half-truths" that keep you from all truth, which is characteristic of satan. Tithing is biblical and is in fact an ancient portal hidden in scripture that was referenced 2,000 years before Jesus was crucified and pre-dates the law of Moses. There are 3 types of tithes in YHWH's system of giving: the church (Levitical priest), the feast offering, and the poor.

CHURCH (Levitical/Priest) - When Abraham (who was called Abram until YHWH changed his name in Genesis 17:5) heard that his nephew Lot was taken captive, he armed his servants who were trained for war, and went in pursuit to rescue him. He and his servants attacked, defeated, and gained victory over Chedorlaomer as well as his allied kings who were with him. He brought back all the goods, along with his nephew Lot and his possessions. Upon their return from the military victory, the king of Sodom came to meet Abraham at the Valley of Shaveh. When there Melchizedek, King of ancient Jerusalem, brought them bread and wine. He also blessed Abraham saying:

> Blessed (joyful, favored) be Abram by YHWH Most High, Creator and Possessor of heaven and earth; And blessed, praised, and glorified be YHWH Most High, Who has given your enemies into your hand." And Abram gave him a tenth of all (the treasure he had taken in battle).
> - GENESIS 14:19-20 (AMP)

Melchizedek, a man who was the priest of YHWH during Abraham's era, was a seven-fold type of Christ. First, he had no recorded pedigree (ancestral line or genealogy) in scripture, making him like unto Christ who is an eternal being (Micah 5:2; Hebrews 7:3,6). Second, he had no recorded birth or death in scripture to demonstrate the endless priesthood of Christ (Psalm 110:4; Hebrews 5:10, 6:20, 7:3, 17, 21, 23-28). Third, he brought forth bread and wine unto Abraham representative of what Christ gave at the Lord's Supper (the Passover meal), exhibiting that he understood atonement and sacrifice (Genesis 14:18; Luke 22:14-20). In addition to this, he had the position of king-priest, which was spoken by Zechariah concerning Christ (Hebrews 7:1; Zechariah 6:12-13). In a like manner, Melchizedek was called by the translation of his name "king of righteousness" and by the translation of the city he ruled over "king of peace" which is comparative to Jesus being called "Prince of Peace" and being made the righteousness of YHWH to us (Isaiah 9:6; I Corinthians 1:30; Hebrews 1:8, 7:2). Lastly, Melchizedek was also greater than Abraham just as Jesus is greater and before Abraham (Hebrews 7:4-8; John 8:54-58). These are all very powerful symbols in scripture that also reveal Christ as a priest appointed forever according to the order of Melchizedek, which was confirmed by YHWH himself (Psalm 110:4; Hebrews 5:6, 6:20, 7:17).

Bearing all these truths in mind, along with the fact that Abraham is the patriarch (the father) of Israel and all who believe, it is the next generations who are to follow in Abraham's example (Romans 4:12). Scripture even lets us know that Levi, the father of the priestly tribe, came out of the loins of Abraham. So even the unborn tribe of Levi, who were charged with the priestly office that were commanded to collect tithes from the people, paid tithes through Abraham (Hebrews 7:5, 9-10). Therefore we, who are grafted into the commonwealth of Israel through the sacrifice of Jesus Christ (who also taught the principle of tithing), are the spiritual seed of Abraham and have access to all his blessings (Matthew 23:23; Luke 11:42; Galatians 3:14; Ephesians 2:9-15). Hence, it was Abraham's obedience to pay tithes that allow us to continue to operate under this same cycle. Abraham brought tithes (translated "tenth" in Hebrew and Greek) to Melchizedek, but Melchizedek was a temporary priest. We have a better covenant with the Lord Jesus Christ (the antitype represented by Melchizedek) by grace through faith. So, He is the one who receives our tithe. The church, which we recognize as the House of God in the natural, is an extension of the Body of Christ. When we bring our tithe to the church, we acknowledge our giving naturally, but Christ receives them spiritually as our High Priest in heaven.

Now, there are some who may still have qualms or issues with tithing, saying it's all about money. If you are one of these people, it shows me that you have one thing but lack another. It shows you have an honor problem and truly lack the spirit of understanding. See, the truth is tithing is not about money at all because it's not even your money. Everything belongs to God. He says even the silver, gold, and cattle on a thousand hills are mine (Psalm 50:10-12; Haggai 2:8). Tithing is an honor principle and it's all about honor to God. When you don't honor YHWH in tithing, you become a thief and a robber. The Bible says:

> [7] Even from the days of your fathers ye are gone away from mine ordinances, and have not kept them. Return unto me, and I will return unto you, saith the LORD of hosts. But ye said, Wherein shall we return? [8] Will a man rob God? Yet ye have robbed me. But ye say, Wherein have we robbed thee? In tithes and offerings. [9] Ye are cursed with a curse: for ye have robbed me, even this whole na-

tion. [10] Bring ye all the tithes into the storehouse, that there may be meat in mine house, and prove me now herewith, saith the LORD of hosts, if I will not open you the windows of heaven, and pour you out a blessing, that there shall not be room enough to receive it. [11] And I will rebuke the devourer for your sakes, and he shall not destroy the fruits of your ground; neither shall your vine cast her fruit before the time in the field, saith the LORD of hosts.

- MALACHI 3:7-11

The storehouse in Israel was not just the temple, but the cities of the Levites. Therefore, to withhold your tithes is not just to rob God, it's robbing a whole nation! The church allows for others to receive help and reaches the masses to preach the gospel of Jesus Christ. One of the main purposes of the church is to evangelize the world and make disciples of all nations. Our commission is to help others learn of Him, believe in Him, and obey His teachings. So, to withhold tithes is to be against the command of YHWH to support the carrying out of his work. This is why, when you rob God, you bring yourself under a curse, open the door for your financial dominion to become stuck, and take away your protection.

Tithing is an ancient portal that opens the door to a level of financial protection provided by YHWH where He places His presence on the 90% because you give Him the 10%. In light of these truths, for you to say that YHWH doesn't want the tenth part is to call YHWH a liar and all you're doing is proving that you are the liar. Numbers 23:19 says, "YHWH is not a man, that he should lie; neither the son of man, that he should repent: hath he said, and shall he not do it? or hath he spoken, and shall he not make it good?" See, YHWH will never allow you to make Him out to be a liar, which is why He tells you to prove Him. So, I charge you today, do what He asked you to do – PROVE HIM. Let YHWH show you exactly who He is!

# CHAPTER TEN

# DOUBLE

> *During these appointed times, His promises and blessings are unlocked for you when you sow your feast offering.*

I n Numbers 28, 29 and 30 it is clear that each month and during the feast times, YHWH commanded offerings were to be made. Giving offerings during these times is a wonderful opportunity because we honor YHWH through our fellowship, which is a portal to His presence during that season. We also honor Him with our substance, which is a seed for continual breakthrough and blessings! As you read this chapter, receive it with joy because the revelations of giving during the moedim (appointed times) are supernatural.

# Types of Offerings

### The Feast Offering

Another hidden portal that is not taught in ministry involves the feast day offerings. The feast offering/second tithe is an additional tithe of one's income saved by the individual each year for use in observing God's holy days. God's holy days are outlined in Leviticus 23, and He commands us on these holy days not to appear before Him empty.

> Three times in a year shall all thy males appear before the Lord thy YHWH in the place which he shall choose; in the feast of unleavened bread, and in the feast of weeks, and in the feast of tabernacles: and they shall not appear before the Lord empty: Every man shall give as he is able, according to the blessing of the Lord thy YHWH which he hath given thee.
> - DEUTERONOMY 16:16-17

Aligning yourself with the seasons and divinely appointed times of YHWH will yield a great harvest. Let's take the seasons of the year for example. When you're in winter, you experience the frigid coldness of the air in winter. When you're in spring, you experience and see the rain and blooming flowers that come in the spring. During that particular time, you experience whatever is predestined to happen in that season. The same thing happens when you celebrate the divinely appointed feasts of the Lord. You get to experience everything that YHWH has divinely appointed for His people during that festival. So, your feast offering becomes the portal whereby you see YHWH pouring out, individually and collectively, supernaturally harvested blessings in real time. Let's look at Passover! It is a time when we celebrate YHWH's love, power, deliverance, grace, and mercy. We praise Him for His past works of deliverance, seek Him for His present deliverance, and gain faith for His future works. This will help you to understand why honoring the Lord with your second tithe is important.

It was commanded that we celebrate Passover both in the Old Testament as well as the New Testament. I Corinthians 5:7-8 tell us, "Clean out the old leaven so that you may be a new batch, just as you are, still unleavened. For Christ our Passover Lamb has been sacrificed. Therefore, let us celebrate the feast, not with old leaven, nor with the leaven of vice and malice and wickedness, but with the unleavened bread of sincerity and (untainted) truth." So, when you celebrate the feast of Passover, you keep it out of relationship with Christ not religion. Hebrews 9:11-14 says:

> But Christ being come an high priest of good things to come, by a greater and more perfect tabernacle, not made with hands, that is to say, not of this building, neither by the blood of goats and calves, but by his own blood he entered in once into the holy place, having obtained eternal redemption for us. For if the blood of bulls and goats, and the ashes of an heifer sprinkling the unclean, sanctifieth to the purifying of the flesh: how much more shall the blood of Christ, who through the eternal spirit offered himself without spot to God, purge your conscience from dead works to serve the living God.

This is why we honor Christ during Passover, for it is the power of His blood that forever compensates for us and purges us in every aspect of our being. Now in celebrating Passover, you have five (5) things that happened and seven (7) supernatural blessings that occur. The 5 things that happened are:

1. By the blood of the lamb, Israel was redeemed.

2. The judgment of YHWH was turned away from the people of Israel.

3. The gods of Egypt were judged, and their powers were taken away.

4. The people of Israel were released from oppression and bondage.

5. The people of Israel were set free to enter God's promise.

These five things that happened to the children of Israel are the same things that will happen for you when you apply the blood of Jesus to your heart. So, if you need vindication, YHWH gives it to you. If anything was siphoned or stolen from you, you begin to recover all. If you have pending cases or judgments against you, YHWH releases you from them. Anyone who is an enemy to your destiny is decimated. If you were denied, you receive an approval and anything that held you captive from the access of YHWH will let you go so that you may enter His promise. Things like this begin to happen suddenly because when you celebrate Passover, seven (7) supernatural blessings are released. These blessings are:

1. YHWH assigns an angel to you (Exodus 23:20).

2. YHWH will be an enemy to your enemies (Exodus 23:22).

3. YHWH will give you prosperity (Exodus 23:25).

4. YHWH takes sickness away from you (Exodus 23:25).

5. YHWH will give you long life (Exodus 23:26).

6. YHWH brings increase and inheritance to you (Exodus 23:30).

7. Special year of blessing (Exodus 23:29).

These are promises YHWH has for you and before He lets His word fall to the ground, He will allow the earth to disintegrate. Why? Because a promise is a promise, and ALL HIS PROMISES ARE YES AND AMEN! So, do you see how special of a time His feasts are? During these appointed times, His promises and blessings are unlocked for you when you sow your feast offering. It becomes your seed in the ground that produces God's supernatural harvest during a special time He calls to meet with His people. And how you know what to give is by taking the time to hear Holy Spirit, carefully listen for His instructions, and obey quickly to give in accordance with what He is saying.

## The Poor

> At Caesarea there was a man named Cornelius, a centurion in what was known as the Italian Regimen. He and all his family were devout and God-fearing; he gave generously to those in need and prayed to YHWH regularly. One day at about three in the afternoon he had a vision. He distinctly saw an angel of God, who came to him and said, "Cornelius!" Cornelius stared at him in fear. "What is it, Lord?" he asked. The angel answered, "Your prayers and gifts to the poor have come up as a memorial before God.
> - ACTS 10:1-4 (NIV)

Giving to the poor is the third tithe, which is also an ancient portal hidden in scripture. It is referenced many times throughout the Bible, revealing that this is something that is precious to the heart of God. Proverbs 19:17 declares that lending to the poor is in fact lending to the Lord, who pays back in full. Again, it is clearly exemplified that what we give physically is received by the Lord spiritually in heaven. In addition to this, the Bible also lets us know that you can be the cause of your own lack by ignoring the needs of the poor and showing no compassion, ultimately displaying that you do not have the love of YHWH living in you (Proverbs 28:27; I John 3:17). Compassion is connected to your attitude and YHWH cares about your attitude when giving to the poor.

Giving to the poor is not something that should be done just to be advertised to others because when you do, you are not reflecting the nature of God. When YHWH does something for you and is working behind the scenes on your behalf, He does it unobtrusively and quietly. When He prepares a table for you or opens doors for you, He does it in love without making a big fuss about it. That's why the Bible says in Psalm 23:5 that He prepares a table for you in the presence of your enemies. He doesn't tell your enemy He's preparing the table; He just goes ahead and does it. You should give to the poor in the same manner. You should not give to be seen by men as in a theatrical performance because you'll get the applause of men, but that's all you'll get. It will not be received by YHWH in heaven because He knows the heart and understands the intent of the thoughts of man. Remember, you should always give out of the love of the heart of the Father. Moreover, giving to the poor is an ancient portal that gives you access to deliverance, protection, blessings, strength, and restoration. In Psalm 41, there is a seven-fold blessing of YHWH attached to giving to the poor. Those who consider the poor will:

1. Be delivered in the time of trouble.
2. Be protected by the Lord.

3. Be kept alive by the Lord.

4. Be called blessed in the land.

5. Be shielded from being overtaken by enemies.

6. Be strengthened by the Lord when sick.

7. Be restored by the Lord back to health.

This portal of tithing to the poor and in turn receiving manifold blessings from heaven in the above passage of scripture is revelatory. When you obey the commands of the Lord, you can always be blessed by YHWH with total abundance that He takes out of eternity and puts into time just for you. You see, giving to the poor is not just about accessing an ancient portal to receive a blessing. It's about laying up treasure in a place not made by the hands of man. When you give away your resources in the natural, you automatically begin to store up treasure in the spirit. It's just like the young ruler who asked Jesus in Luke 18 what he shall do to inherit eternal life and Jesus told him that he forgot one command - to sell all his possessions and distribute it to the poor. Only then would he have abundant treasure in heaven. Eternal life doesn't start when you die, it starts right now! Therefore, when you obey YHWH and give consistent with His commands, your eternal treasures stored up in heaven boomerang back to its eternal homing device, causing you to never run dry here in the earth.

## Firstfruit

> Honor the LORD with your wealth And with the first fruits of all
> your crops (income); Then your barns will be abundantly filled
> And your vats will overflow with new wine."
> - PROVERBS 3:9-10 (AMP)

It is extremely important to give YHWH the first portion of all of your income. It commands a blessing of YHWH on your finances that cannot be revoked. This is an ancient portal that aligns with the ancient portal of Rosh Chodesh, that when followed, brings a blessing over your whole month, an impartation of divine intelligence, and rapid release of supernatural ideas. Honoring the Lord with the first portion of your finances at the head of every Hebraic month will cause your mind to be abundantly implanted with an influx of new strategies and blueprints from heaven that will cause you to live in the surplus of God. This is a place where you have reserves of what you need because you are divinely connected to a surge of power from heaven through the dual alignment of two (2) ancient portals. In addition to this, you can experience the holiness of YHWH resting on your finances for the entire year. In Romans 11:16, the Bible declares, *For if the first fruit is holy, the lump is also holy; and if the root is holy, so are the branches.*

Jesus is the first fruit of the dead and He is holy. Therefore, you honor Him with the first of your increase so that your finances can be connected to the holiness of YHWH because what's in the root is also in the branches. When God's holiness becomes the root of your finances, it permeates into your monetary flow throughout the rest of your year. You are essentially allowing YHWH to create an impenetrable shield of His favor around your finances. Not only will this happen for you, but you also position yourself to have a blessing on your home. The Bible says in Ezekiel:

> The first of all first fruits of every kind and every contribution
> of every kind, from all your contributions, shall be for the priests:
> you shall also give to the priest the first of your dough to cause a
> blessing on the rest of your house.
> - EZEKIEL 44:30 (NAS)

When this scripture above says the "*rest of your house*", it literally means everyone in your entire house! Just like when the Ark of the Covenant sat in the house of Obededom for three months and his house was blessed, that's what happens when you sow your first fruit seed. Everything attached to you is blessed. So that means both your saved and unsaved loved ones benefit from your seed also, which goes beyond financial need. Many times, a financial blessing is not our main concern. There are many other non-monetary needs that this blessing extends to such as emotional, spiritual, and physical healing for you and your family. So, it's not about money, it's about a seed being able to break a cycle. When a woman gets pregnant due to the implanting of the seed of a man within her, her recurring monthly cycle stops. What am I saying? Put your first fruit seed in the ground to do away with old patterns, establish new heavenly patterns, and become the production center for mind blowing testimonies from heaven. Why? Because,

# It's time for full realignment so that you can partake in all that the Father has for you!

# CONCLUSION

## Realignment

This book was not written just to reveal certain portals and principles hidden in scripture. This book is a call-to-action from the Lord. This is a divine summoning to be effective as an ambassador of heaven, live a kingdom lifestyle, operate in heaven's economy, and access holy portals and the things of YHWH so you can live a completely transformed intimate life with the Holy Spirit. It's a call to full realignment with the Kingdom of God, His principles, His protocols, and His agenda. IT'S A DIVINE CALL TO YOU!

YHWH called us to be of Himself, not of the world. The world cannot be a better place when you operate out of it. When you're living under the rule and guise of the kingdom of darkness, you're consistently accessing satanic portals and subsequently satanic things. Always know, you cannot give out of the pure heart of Christ if you operate out of the heart of satan and fulfill satanic mandates. When you fulfill a satanic mandate by operating according to his rules, suggestions, and commands, you're not living out of the original mandate that YHWH strategically called you to, which hinders you from walking in real dominion. You're letting something or someone else dictate who you are and write out your destiny. So, if throughout reading this book, you've recognized that you have not been in full alignment with YHWH in various areas of your life or have been involved in somethings that has taken you out of the will of the Father, it is imperative that you know the Lord is calling you higher and wants to use you in an even greater way.

However, He cannot use a contaminated vessel. He needs you to come into a realm called "empty", so you can ascend to a dimension called "available". You must get empty before Him of all the things in your life characteristic of satan's kingdom so that you can ascend to His dimension of availability where He can use the totality of your being (spirit, soul, and body) effectively for His glory. He is seeking this very moment to put you on the right page of your destiny book where you are holy, whole, free, and prosperous!

Therefore, there is no better time than RIGHT NOW to come into full alignment with the Kingdom of God. It is time to come out of whatever you have found yourself in that doesn't pertain to life and godliness and has kept you out of His system of living and cycle of blessings.

So...

- *If you're operating, teaching, or preaching out of religion, come out.*

- *If you're celebrating satanic holidays, come out.*

- *If you're living a life of prayerlessness, come out.*

- *If you don't honor God's Holy days, come out.*

- *If you're not giving your resources (financial & non-financial) to advance the Kingdom agenda, come out.*

- *If you have no compassion on the poor, come out.*

- *If you're accepting sickness and disease as your portion or your children's portion, come out.*

- *If you're living in poverty in your mind, come out.*

- *If you're walking in pride, come out.*

- *If you're making things, technology, places, or people your God, come out.*

- *If you have friendships that keep you blind, weak, lazy, docile, or in sin, come out.*

- *If you're disrespecting your spouse, come out.*

- *If you're treating your children wrong, come out.*

- *If you're dishonoring your parents, come out.*

- *If you're living in rejection, come out.*

- *If you're living in abandonment, come out.*

- *If you're an abuser or living in an abusive situation, come out.*

- *If you're living out of what happened to you as a child, come out.*

- *If you're living in fear, worry, anxiety, depression, oppression, or low self-esteem, come out.*

- *If you gossip, murder, or have a murderous tongue, come out.*

- *If you're living in jealousy, hatred, or unforgiveness, come out.*

- *If you're speaking vulgar words, come out.*

- *If you're a manipulator, come out.*

- *If you're a know-it-all, come out.*

- *If you're living in offense, come out.*

- *If you're living in anger and bitterness, come out.*

I could go on and on, but you get the picture! It's time to come out an any and everything that does not reflect the Kingdom of God. Come out by repenting and renouncing any satanic portal you've accessed and anything you've done to align yourself with the kingdom of darkness. Close the door forever and seal it by the blood of Jesus! Once you've done that and rededicated your life fully back to God, you can now effectively: operate as a new species in Christ

Jesus; fully access holy portals; carry the brilliance and glory of YHWH on everything you have and wherever you go; change the trajectory of your life, legislate and adjudicate on behalf of heaven; walk in the authority and power of Yahushua HaMashiach (Jesus Christ); and declare God's wisdom in the Earth. Why? Because a life lived intimately with the precious Holy Spirit, through the blood of Jesus, and in accordance with our heavenly Father's teachings is a true joyous, successful, abundant, eternal life!

# ADDITIONAL RESOURCES

This section provides easy to access references for you as you seek to realign yourself with your Hebraic roots. As you do so, you will find that portals will constantly open for you to access YHWH. You will walk in perpetual cycles of the blessings and the supernatural. As the scripture has said, "… signs shall follow them that believe."

## TETRAGRAM - YHWH

Some scholars have concluded, based on the study of original Hebrew and ancient writings, that the true name of Our Father in Heaven, Elohim, also called Hashem (The Name) is the four-letter tetragrammaton. It appears only as four consonant letters, YHWH (Hebrew, Yod Heh Wau Heh, read right to left). Note that there were no vowels in the original writing. The spoken name of YHWH is considered very powerful by the sages. It has been kept secret for centuries and is now being revealed to the Body of Christ in these end times to help like the Israelites who called upon His name in ancient times and experienced the supernatural power or YHWH.

**BEHOLD NAIL BEHOLD HAND**

יהוה

**YHWH**

| Ancient Semitic/Hebrew | | | | | | | Modern Hebrew | | | Greek | | Latin |
|---|---|---|---|---|---|---|---|---|---|---|---|---|
| Early | Middle | Late | Name | Picture | Meaning | Sound | Letter | Name | Sound | Ancient | Modern | |
| 𐤀 | ✝𝑥 | א | El | Ox head | Strong, Power, Leader | ah, eh | א | Aleph | [silent] | A | A | A |
| 𐤁 | 𝑔 | 𐤁 | Bet | Tent floorplan | Family, House, In | b, bh(v) | ב | Beyt | b, bh(v) | B | B | B |
| ✓ | 𐤂 | ג | Gam | Foot | Gather, Walk | g | ג | Gimal | g | Γ | Γ | C G |
| ▽ | ◁ | 𐤃 | Dal | Door | Move, Hang, Entrance | d | ד | Dalet | d | Δ | Δ | D |
| Ψ | 𝟃 | 𐤄 | Hey | Man with arms raised | Look, Reveal, Breath | h, ah | ה | Hey | h | E | E | E |
| Y | 𐤅 | ו | Waw | Tent peg | Add, Secure, Hook | w, o, u | ו | Vav | v | F | | F |
| 𝓕 | 𝓕 | ו | Zan | Mattock | Food, Cut, Nourish | z | ז | Zayin | z | Z | Z | Z |
| 𐤇 | 𐤇 | 𐤇 | Hhet | Tent wall | Wall, Outside, Divide, Half | hh | ח | Chet | hh | H | H | H |
| ⊗ | ⊗ | ט | Tet | Basket | Surround, Contain, Mud | t | ט | Tet | t | Θ | Θ | |
| 𐤉 | 𝓨 | ׳ | Yad | Arm and closed hand | Hand, Work, Throw, Worship | y, ee | י | Yud | y | I | I | I J |
| 𐤊 | 𝑦 | כ | Kaph | Open palm | Bend, Open, Allow, Tame | k, kh | כ | Kaph | k, kh | K | K | K |
| ∠ | 𝓁 | ל | Lam | Shepherd Staff | Teach, Yoke, Authority, Bind | l | ל | Lamed | l | Λ | Λ | L |
| ᴟ | 𝑦 | מ | Mem | Water | Water, Chaos, Mighty, Blood | m | מ | Mem | m | M | M | M |
| ⟍ | 𝑦 | נ | Nun | Seed | Seed, Continue, Heir, Son | n | נ | Nun | n | N | N | N |
| 𐤎 | 𐤎 | ס | Sin | Thorn | Grab, Hate, Protect | s | ס | Samech | s | Ξ | Ξ | X |
| ⊙ | O | ע | An | Eye | See, Watch, Know, Shade | [silent] | ע | Ayin | [silent] | O | O | O |
| 𐤏 | O | ע | Ghah | Rope | Twist, Dark, Wicked | gh | | | | | | |
| ⟍ | 𝑦 | פ | Pey | Mouth | Open, Blow, Scatter, Edge | p, ph(f) | פ | Pey | p, ph(f) | Π | Π | P |
| 𝞱 | 𝑟 | צ | Tsad | Trail | Trail, Journey, Chase, Hunt | ts | צ | Tsade | ts | Ϻ | | |
| 𐤒 | 𐤒 | ק | Quph | Sun on the horizon | Condense, Circle, Time | q | ק | Quph | q | Ϙ | | Q |
| 𐤓 | 𐤓 | ר | Resh | Head of a man | Head, First, Top, Beginning | r | ר | Resh | r | Ρ | Ρ | R |
| 𐤔 | w | ש | Shin | Two front teeth | Sharp, Press, Eat, Two | sh | ש | Shin Sin | sh, s | Σ | Σ | S |
| ✝ | ✕ | ת | Taw | Crossed sticks | Mark, Sign, Signal, Monument | t | ת | Tav | t | T | T | T |

# Hebrew/Gregorian Calendar

This calendar shows when the Hebrew months fall relative to the months on the Gregorian calendar. Note: All the names for the Hebrew months originate from the Israelites time in Babylonian captivity. Originally, the months had no name, only numbers, i.e. the 1st month, the 2nd month, the 3rd month and so on. Some names have various spelling in English, i.e. Nissan vs Nisan and Iyar vs Iyyar.

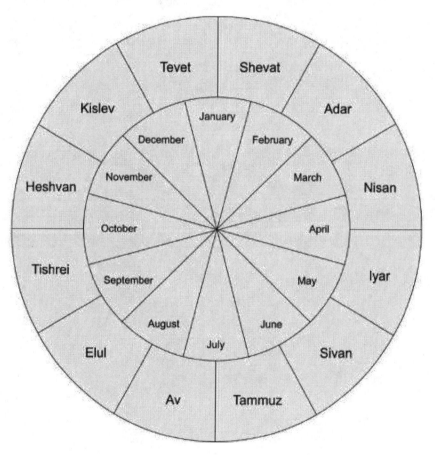

# Constellations

Each month has a constellation/sign assigned to it. There are 12 constellations together referred to as the zodiac or "Mazzaroth" in Hebrew. The following are the Biblical representations for each constellation.

1. **The Maiden (Virgo).** VIRGIN MARY - This constellation depicts Yahushua (Jesus), born of a virgin, as the first born of many brethren (wheat).

2. **The Scales (Libra).** REPRESENTS THE WEIGHT OF SIN - This constellation depicts Christ as our redeemer, paying the full price for our sin.

3. **The Scorpion (Scorpius).** SIN BRINGS DEATH – Its sting is the death of Christ, but as promised He will bruise satan's head and gain the final victory, which will be over death itself.

4. **The Archer (Sagittarius).** DEMONISM - This constellation reveals the conflict between good and evil and the conquering Christ who was both human and divine swiftly defeating the enemy.

5. **The Sea-Goat (Capricornus).** EARTH's CORRUPTION - This constellation reveals Christ as the sacrificial lamb and His resurrection. It also speaks to dying to sin, repentance, which brings salvation, new life.

6. **The Water Bearer (Aquarius).** LIVING WATER - This constellation depicts Christ pouring out the revelation of the Kingdom on His church. "It is believed the Kingdom will be poured out in three phases, Passover, Pentecost, and Tabernacles. [26]" Christ is the living water.

7. **The Fishes (Pisces).** YHWH's REMNANT - The church and overcomers - This constellation depicts the church who seems to be losing the battle against satan but will triumph over evil. This constellation signifies humanity's need for YHWH's Holy Spirit.

8. **The Ram (Aries).** CHRIST WAS OUR SACRIFICE – This constellation speaks of the marriage supper of the Lamb and reveals that He is Lord over both Jew and Gentile, and all mankind.

9. **The Bull (Taurus).** STRENGTH - This constellation represents the feast of tabernacles where 70 bulls were sacrificed, how Christ will crush the enemy with great force, and the Millennial reign.

10. **The Twins (Gemini).** CHRISTS DUAL NATURE – He is both Son of YHWH and Son of Man

11. **The Crab (Cancer).** PROTECTION – This constellation depicts that Christ provides safety and rest for His beloved (His Bride the Church).

12. **The Lion (Leo).** THE KING – This constellation shows that Christ will rule forever.

# Hebraic Symbols Associated With Each Month

Each month has a tribe, stone, constellation, letter, sense, and organ associated with it. By searching the Bible each month to find the significance of these symbolic associations you will receive revelations into what YHWH is speaking to you as an individual and to the Body of Christ as a whole.

| | |
|---|---|
| Hebrew Month | **Tishrei** |
| Gregorian Calendar | September/October |
| Tribe | Ephraim |
| Stone | Jacinth |
| Constellation | Libra |
| Alphabet | Lamed |
| Sense | Touch |
| Organ | Gallbladder |

| | |
|---|---|
| Hebrew Month | **Cheshvan** |
| Gregorian Calendar | October/November |
| Tribe | Manasseh |
| Stone | Agate |
| Constellation | Scorpio |
| Alphabet | Nun |
| Sense | Smell |
| Organ | Intestines |

| Hebrew Month | **Kislev** |
|---:|:---|
| Gregorian Calendar | November/December |
| Tribe | Benjamin |
| Stone | Amethyst |
| Constellation | Sagittarius |
| Alphabet | Samech |
| Sense | Sleep/Dreams |
| Organ | Abdomen/Belly |

| Hebrew Month | **Tevet** |
|---:|:---|
| Gregorian Calendar | December/January |
| Tribe | Dan |
| Stone | Beryl Stone |
| Constellation | Capricorn |
| Alphabet | Ayin |
| Sense | Anger |
| Organ | Liver |

| Hebrew Month | **Shevat** |
|---:|:---|
| Gregorian Calendar | January/February |
| Tribe | Asher |
| Stone | Onyx |
| Constellation | Aquarius |
| Alphabet | Tzadik |
| Sense | Taste |

| Hebrew Month | **Adar** |
|---|---|
| Gregorian Calendar | February/March |
| Tribe | Naphtali |
| Stone | Jasper |
| Constellation | Pisces |
| Alphabet | Kaf |
| Sense | Laughter |
| Organ | Spleen |

| Hebrew Month | **Nissan** |
|---|---|
| Gregorian Calendar | March/April |
| Tribe | Judah |
| Stone | Sardis |
| Constellation | Aries |
| Alphabet | Hey |
| Sense | Speech |
| Organ | Right Foot |

| Hebrew Month | **Iyar** |
|---|---|
| Gregorian Calendar | April/May |
| Tribe | Issachar |
| Stone | Topaz |
| Constellation | Taurus |
| Alphabet | Vav |
| Sense | Thought |
| Organ | Kidneys |

| Hebrew Month | **Sivan** |
| --- | --- |
| Gregorian Calendar | May/June |
| Tribe | Zebulun |
| Stone | Carbuncle |
| Constellation | Gemini |
| Alphabet | Zayin |
| Sense | Walking |
| Organ | Left Foot |

| Hebrew Month | **Tammuz** |
| --- | --- |
| Gregorian Calendar | June/July |
| Tribe | Reuben |
| Stone | Emerald |
| Constellation | Cancer |
| Alphabet | Chet |
| Sense | Sight |
| Organ | Right Hand |

| Hebrew Month | **Av** |
| --- | --- |
| Gregorian Calendar | July/August |
| Tribe | Simeon |
| Stone | Sapphire |
| Constellation | Leo |
| Alphabet | Tet |
| Sense | Hearing |
| Organ | Left Kidney |

| | |
|---|---|
| Hebrew Month | **Elul** |
| Gregorian Calendar | August/September |
| Tribe | Gad |
| Stone | Diamond |
| Constellation | Virgo |
| Alphabet | Yod |
| Sense | Action |
| Organ | Left Hand |

# The Annual Feasts of the LORD

Each of the seven feasts have a historical fulfillment, prophetic significance, and a spiritual application. The four spring feasts have already been fulfilled with the death, burial, resurrection and giving of Holy Spirit. We are in earnest expectation of the fulfillment of the last three feasts which will consummate the return of the Lord, the judgment, and the millennial reign.

# The Three Spring Feasts Outlined:

*Passover*
Historical Fulfillment: Israel's deliverance out of Egypt
Prophetic Significance: Christ's death
Spiritual Application: Salvation

*Unleavened Bread*
Historical Fulfillment: From Egypt into the Red Sea
Prophetic Significance: Christ's burial
Spiritual Application: Water Baptism

*First Fruits*
Historical Fulfillment: Coming out of the Red Sea
Prophetic Significance: Christ's resurrection
Spiritual Application: Resurrected new life in Christ

# The Feasts Just Before Summer:

*Pentecost*

Historical Fulfillment: Giving of the Torah; Birth of the nation

Prophetic Significance: Giving of Holy Spirit; Birth of the Church

Spiritual Application: Baptism in Holy Spirit

# Three Fall Feasts Outlined:

*Trumpets:*

Historical Fulfillment: Call to possess the Promised Land

Prophetic Significance: Messiah as Deliverer

Spiritual Application: Resurrection and Rapture

*Atonement:*

Historical Fulfillment: National cleansing & consecration

Prophetic Significance: Messiah as High Priest

Spiritual Application: Full Redemption

*Tabernacles*

Historical Fulfillment: Possessing the Promised Land

Prophetic Significance: Messiah as King (Millennial Reign)

Spiritual Application: Full rest in YHWH

# REFERENCES

1   Jeff A. Benner, "A Short History of the Hebrew Language: AHRC," *A Short History of the Hebrew Language | AHRC*, https://ancient-hebrew.org/language/short-history-of-the-hebrew-language.htm.

2   Ari Sorko-Ram and Shira Sorko-Ram, "Father of the Modern Hebrew Language - Sid Roth – It's Supernatural!" *Sid Roth – It's Supernatural!* | Sidroth.org, 11 Sept. 2018, https://sidroth.org/articles/father-of-the-modern-hebrew-language/.

3   Dustin Herron, "What Are the Moedim? the 7 Appointed Times," *FIRM Israel*, 22 Aug. 2022, https://firmisrael.org/learn/what-are-the-moedim/#:~:text=The%20plural%20form%20of%20"mo,preset%20appointed%20time%20has%20come.

4   "Glossary - Moedim." Psalm11918. Org, https://www.psalm11918.org/References/Glossary/moedim.html.

5   *Hjem/Home*, http://www.nordiskisrael.dk/.

6   My Jewish Learning. "7 Things You Should Know about Hebrew." *My Jewish Learning*, 11 Oct. 2017, https://www.myjewishlearning.com/article/the-hebrew-language/.

7   Delightful Knowledge, "The Hidden Name of the Creator in Your DNA," *Delightful Knowledge*, 1 Nov. 2014, http://www.delightfulknowledge.com/hidden-name-of-creator-in-your-dna.

8   "Who Is Larry Ellison? Everything You Need to Know," *Facts, Childhood, Family Life & Achievements*, https://www.thefamouspeople.com/profiles/larry-ellison-4932.php.

9   "What Natural Resources Are Present in the Middle East?" *Reference, IAC Publishing*, https://www.reference.com/geography/natural-resources-present-middle-east-1832c95dd7b21245.

10   "The Paleo-Hebrew Alphabet: AHRC." *The Paleo-Hebrew Alphabet* | AHRC, https://www.ancient-hebrew.org/ancient-alphabet/paleo-hebrew-alphabet.htm.

11   "Hebrew and Greek Alphabet and Numerical Values," *Divisions Structure Bible Menorah*, https://menorah-bible.jimdofree.com/english/structure-of-the-bible/alphabets-and-numerical-values/.

12   "The Jewish Cover Up: 'Don't Mention the Set-Apart Name!'"." *Chapter 2*, http://www.yahushua.net/YAHUWAH/chapter_02.htm.

13 MCBCHS2014. "The English Language Is Full of Spells & Curses!" YouTube, *YouTube*, 27 Aug. 2018, https://www.youtube.com/watch?v=ZvBTHl_hzz8.

14 "A Short History of the Hebrew Language: AHRC," *A Short History of the Hebrew Language | AHRC*, https://ancient-hebrew.org/language/short-history-of-the-hebrew-language.htm.

15 "Secret Spells of the English Language," YouTube, *YouTube*, 27 Oct. 2015, https://www.youtube.com/watch?v=35cnsY6jb9s&t=29s.

16 Mark Roberts, "What Language Did Jesus Speak? Why Does It Matter?" *Patheos*, 25 Jan. 2014, https://www.patheos.com/blogs/markdroberts/series/what-language-did-jesus-speak-why-does-it-matter/.

17 *GotQuestions.org*, 19 Oct. 2020, https://www.gotquestions.org/come-out-of-her.html.

18 BibleAsk, "Did Paul Keep the Seventh Day Sabbath?" *BibleAsk*, 27 June 2022, https://bibleask.org/did-paul-keep-the-seventh-day-sabbath/.

19 BibleAsk, "Did Paul Keep the Seventh Day Sabbath?" *BibleAsk*, 27 June 2022, https://bibleask.org/did-paul-keep-the-seventh-day-sabbath/.

20 BibleAsk, "Did Paul Keep the Seventh Day Sabbath?" BibleAsk, 27 June 2022, https://bibleask.org/did-paul-keep-the-seventh-day-sabbath/.

21 *Miami Breaking News, Sports, Crime & More | Miami Herald.* https://www.miamiherald.com/.

22 *Rosh Chodesh (First Restoration),* https://www.torahwayoflife.com/rosh_chodesh.

23 "The Biblical New Year," *The Israel Bible*, 24 Feb. 2022, https://theisraelbible.com/the-biblical-new-year/.

24 "The Biblical New Year," *The Israel Bible*, 24 Feb. 2022, https://theisraelbible.com/the-biblical-new-year/.

25 "The Biblical New Year," *The Israel Bible*, 24 Feb. 2022, https://theisraelbible.com/the-biblical-new-year/.

26 "Aquarius," *Bible Study Lessons, Trivia, Verses, and Fellowship*, http://www.bible-study-lessons.com/Aquarius.html.

# ABOUT
# THE AUTHOR

Dr. Sharon R. Nesbitt is simply a lover of God and a lover of people! While serving as a coveted spiritual leader, author, philanthropist and humanitarian, Dr. Nesbitt has founded several works to include Dominion World Outreach Ministries located in Marion, Arkansas, Dominion World Development Corporation and Dominion World Guatemala. Additionally, Dr. Nesbitt's entrepreneurial anointing has led and directed the acquisition, purchase and development of land and facilities on behalf of the ministry. The most recent purchase, 102 acres of land, will house the new Dominion campus.

These efforts, along with her integral character, unparalleled leadership, and decades of dedication to teaching spiritual truths, has led to her being honored with several prestigious awards to include the Presidential Lifetime Achievement and Volunteer Service Award, as well as being appointed Goodwill Ambassador for the Golden Rule under the Interfaith Peace Building Initiative.

Dr. Nesbitt's personal passion is to see people move beyond cultural and socioeconomic barriers and flow in their God-given purpose. As she travels domestically and internationally ministering across racial and denominational boundaries, Dr. Nesbitt continues to sow seeds that will produce a harvest of transformation for generations to come.

# OTHER PUBLICATIONS

**THE SEVEN FORCES OF SUPERNATURAL FAITH**
In this book, Dr. Sharon Nesbitt reveals seven forces of faith that will launch you into the supernatural. Offering an in-depth analysis of each force, she shows you how to unlock the supernatural endowments of faith and develop it from a substance into a servant that accesses miraculous manifestation on your behalf.

**SCARLET STREAM** — *Unveiling the Mystery; Releasing the Supernatural*
Explains the supernatural quality of Jesus' blood as the foundation and culmination of the miraculous. By tracing the incorporation of blood in Scripture from Adam to Christ, and by highlighting the significance of communion in the lives of believers today, she interweaves God's intention for supernatural living with the appropriation of Jesus' blood. As she discusses the seven areas at which that blood was shed, Dr. Nesbitt outlines God's plan to reactivate the intent of Eden by shifting humanity from fall into fellowship.

**CHOSEN FOR GREATNESS** — *Discovering Your Dominion Mandate*
Speaks to the heart of every individual who knows that life was meant to be more than what he/she experiences on a daily basis. The quest for understanding of purpose makes this a must read for all believers.

**SEEDS** — *Daily Decrees That Bring Dominion*
Explains the power of the spoken Word in the areas of Family, Health, Wealth, Soul Winning, Leadership, etc.

**SEEDS FOR DIVINE HEALTH**
The Word of God in the heart and mouth of the believer is the most creative force in the universe. This book provides a strategic outline for understanding the power of the God's word and applying it to everyday life through confession. This expanded series of Seeds focuses on daily decrees that bring dominion to the Health of every believer.

**SEEDS FOR COVENANT WEALTH**
Dr. Nesbitt shares revelation that exposes the lies of the enemy and digs up the root of poverty that plagues believers everywhere. She gives the reader solutions and daily tools that if applied, will transform the mind and bring the manifestation of covenant wealth that God intends for his people to have.

TO ORDER, WRITE OR CALL:

**Sharon R. Nesbitt Ministries**

P. O. Box 41

Marion, AR 72364

Phone: (870) 739-1331 Toll Free: (866) 579-5807

Email: info@dominionworld.org

Web Address: www.dominionworld.org

# YOUR
## *Prophetic*
## C O M M U N I T Y

Sign up for a **FREE** subscription to the Destiny Image digital magazine and get awesome content delivered directly to your inbox!

**destinyimage.com/signup**

## Sign up for Cutting-Edge Messages that Supernaturally Empower You

- Gain valuable insights and guidance based on biblical principles
- Deepen your faith and understanding of God's plan for your life
- Receive regular updates and prophetic messages
- Connect with a community of believers who share your values and beliefs

## Experience Fresh Video Content that Reveals Your Prophetic Inheritance

- Receive prophetic messages and insights
- Connect with a powerful tool for spiritual growth and development
- Stay connected and inspired on your faith journey

## Listen to Powerful Podcasts that Propel You into God's Presence Every Day

- Deepen your understanding of God's prophetic assignment
- Experience God's revival power throughout your day
- Learn how to grow spiritually in your walk with God

# In the Right Hands, This Book Will Change Lives!

Most of the people who need this message will not be looking for this book. To change their lives, you need to **put a copy of this book in their hands.**

Our ministry is constantly seeking methods to find the people who need this anointed message to change their lives. **Will you help us reach these people?**

**Extend this ministry by sowing three, five, ten, or *even more* books today and change people's lives for the better!** Your generosity will be part of catalyzing the Great Awakening that many have been prophesying and praying for.

From

# Sid Roth

## So this is Heaven!

These true stories are your unique, personal opportunities to enjoy a taste of Heaven from here on earth. *Heaven Is Beyond Your Wildest Expectations* shares the testimonies of ten ordinary people who have been to Heavenhaving died and returned, or in a vision or dream.

These real-life, modern-day stories inspire faith that, no matter what happens here on earth, all troubles are momentary, light afflictions compared to the glory that awaits you in Heaven. *For momentary, light affliction is producing for us an eternal weight of glory far beyond all comparison* (2 Corinthians 4:17).

When you see God's love permeating all of Heaven and realize that He reaches down to you right where you are, your heart will come to rest in Him-knowing He is watching over you and that His angels will minister to you in every moment of need. When you know that Heaven's splendor and glory is your eternal destiny, you can endure whatever you must while patiently waiting for the day when you will enter Heaven and your eternal joy in the presence of the Lord.

## Purchase your copy wherever books are sold.

From

# Sid Roth

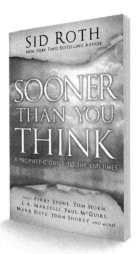

## Your Prophetic Handbook to End-Times Events!

Sid Roth, host of *It's Supernatural!*, has gathered some of the leading experts and prophetic voices to take you on a powerful journey of upcoming events.

Each author shares a different part of the prophetic puzzle. By the time you finish reading this book, the pieces will come together and create a clear picture of God's unfolding agenda for the end-times.

Discover how this pivotal moment in history is your great opportunity to be on guard against the enemy's deception, experience God's power like never before, and participate in the greatest revival in history!

## Purchase your copy wherever books are sold.